What Really Matters

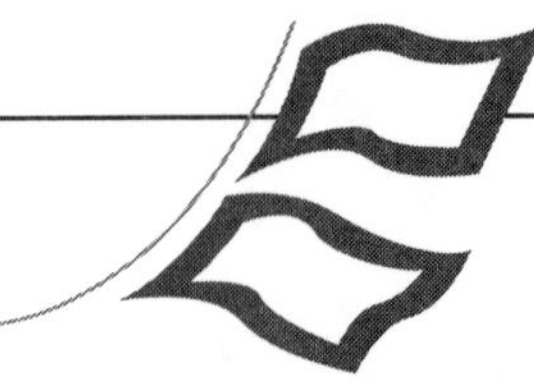

Flagship church resources

from Group Publishing

Innovations From Leading Churches

Flagship Church Resources are your shortcut to innovative and effective leadership ideas. You'll find ideas for every area of church leadership including pastoral ministry, adult ministry, youth ministry, and children's ministry.

Flagship Church Resources are created by the leaders of thriving, dynamic, and trend-setting churches around the country. These nationally recognized teaching churches host regional leadership conferences and are respected by other pastors and church leaders because their approaches to ministry are so effective. These flagship church resources reveal the proven ideas, programs, and principles that these churches have put into practice.

Flagship Church Resources currently available:

- ***60 Simple Secrets Every Pastor Should Know***
- ***The Perfectly Imperfect Church:*** *Redefining the "Ideal Church"*
- ***The Winning Spirit:*** *Empowering Teenagers Through God's Grace*
- ***Ultimate Skits:*** *20 Parables for Driving Home Your Point*
- ***Doing Life With God:*** *Real Stories Written by Students*
- ***Doing Life With God 2:*** *Real Stories Written by Students*
- ***The Visual Edge:*** *Compelling Video Connectors for Your Worship Experience*
- ***Mission-Driven Worship:*** *Helping Your Changing Church Celebrate God*
- ***An Unstoppable Force:*** *Daring to Become the Church God Had in Mind*
- ***A Follower's Life:*** *12 Group Studies On What It Means to Walk With Jesus*
- ***Leadership Essentials for Children's Ministry***
- ***Keeping Your Head Above Water:*** *Refreshing Insights for Church Leadership*
- ***Seeing Beyond Church Walls:*** *Action Plans for Touching Your Community*
- ***unLearning Church:*** *Just When You Thought You Had Leadership all Figured Out!*
- ***Morph!:*** *The Texture of Leadership for Tomorrow's Church*
- ***The Quest for Christ:*** *Discipling Today's Young Adults*
- ***LeadingIdeas:*** *To-the-Point Training for Christian Leaders*
- ***Igniting Passion in Your Church:*** *Becoming Intimate With Christ*
- ***No More Lone Rangers:*** *How to Build a Team-Centered Youth Ministry*
- ***What Really Matters:*** *30 Devotions for Church Leadership Teams*
- ***Children's Ministry Leadership:*** *The You-Can-Do-It Guide*

With more to follow!

What Really Matters

30 DEVOTIONS for CHURCH LEADERSHIP TEAMS

by **Mike Foss**
and **Terri Elton**

Flagship church resources
from Group Publishing

30 DEVOTIONS FOR CHURCH LEADERSHIP TEAMS

Visit our Web site: **www.grouppublishing.com**

CREDITS
Creative Development Editor: Paul Woods
Chief Creative Officer: Joani Schultz
Editor: Candace McMahan
Copy Editor: Lyndsay E. Gerwing
Book Designer: Jean Bruns
Print Production Artist: Stephen Beer
Cover Art Director: Jeff A. Storm
Cover Designer and Photographer: Liz Howe
Production Manager: Peggy Naylor

LIBRARY OF CONGRESS CATALOGING-IN-PUBLICATION DATA
Foss, Michael W., 1948-
What really matters : 30 devotions for church leadership teams / by Michael W. Foss and Terri Martinson Elton.
p. cm.
ISBN 0-7644-2449-1 (pbk. : alk. paper)
1. Christian leadership--Prayer-books and devotions--English. I. Elton, Terri Martinson, 1964- II. Title.
BV652.1.F67 2003
242'.69--dc21
2003000713
Revised

10 9 8 7 6 5 4 3 2 1 12 11 10 09 08 07 06 05 04 03

Printed in the United States of America.

TABLE OF CONTENTS

Section Four

RAISING UP LEADERS AROUND YOU

Section Five

CONFLICT AND CHANGE

INTRODUCTION

The crisis in the church in our time is a crisis of leadership. The old mechanisms for identifying, growing, and commissioning leaders have failed us. We hope that this book will, in a small way, help correct this problem.

We have worked together at Prince of Peace in Burnsville, Minnesota, for nearly ten years. During that time we have shared a passion for leadership development. This has led us to identify discipleship as the context within which leaders are best developed. With discipleship as our focus, we have been called back to living and learning within the context of God's Word. As we've claimed the power of God's Word in our everyday leadership journeys, we've experienced a deeper calling to prayer. Not surprisingly, these two disciplines lead us to truth-telling. Truth-telling means not only speaking difficult truths to others but also facing the hard truths about leadership and our own faith journeys. When we do this, we stop talking about faith and begin to not only live it but also embody it in how we lead. As leaders embody their faith, God uses them to produce other leaders.

As we have grown in our understanding of the leadership journey, we've discovered that leaders not only work best within teams, they also learn and grow more deeply and fully within teams. Teams may be formal work groups, informal collegial groups, small groups, or ministry partners. In any case, when leaders discover the power of a team, they also find the freedom to lean on others' gifts and passions. Then the work that can be so burdensome and isolating shows them that Christ is indeed present, both within themselves and within the group. This takes learning "beyond the head"; it becomes life changing.

So we invite you into a personal encounter with God's Word that you can then share in other contexts with your leadership team. First, use the devotions, written by Mike Foss, for your own personal spiritual growth and grounding. Read and reflect upon them privately, well in advance of meeting with your team. Then use the exercises following each devotion to equip or train your team. Terri Elton has designed these experiential learning opportunities to spark greater dialogue about the Scripture passages and to help participants find the passages' relevance to their lives.

The book is designed for maximum flexibility. The devotions and exercises may be used independently of each other. You may work through the devotions in sequence or focus on issues of special concern or interest. The devotions and exercises may be used in a wide variety of settings and with teams of all types. For example, you might consider using them to transform your church council into a body that invests meaningful time in discipleship and spiritual growth in addition to tending to the business of the church.

Through this book, we invite you and your teammates to share our leadership journey. In the process, we hope God will lead you to deeper insights into his purpose for you and those with whom you share the privilege and burden of leadership.

—Mike Foss and Terri Elton

Section One
PERSONAL DISCIPLESHIP

I have never met a Christian leader, whether clergy, staff, or non-staff leader, who has entered into leadership in the church because he or she liked managing. Nor have I ever met a leader who signed on for ministry because he or she sought prestige or power. I *have* met countless Christian leaders whose positions in the church were the result of a personal encounter with Jesus Christ.

Leadership is an extension of the personal discipleship of Christian men and women. It is the expression of their service in obedience to Jesus Christ.

But, between that experience and their expression of faith through leadership, the business of the ministry can crowd out personal spiritual practices. Worship can become either something leaders do for others or something they do out of obligation. Bible reading and prayer can easily become perfunctory or done on the run. When the very source of our calling is ignored or pushed to the sidelines of our lives, we burn out, rust out, or simply suffer shrinkage of the soul.

Everything begins and ends with our personal relationship with the Savior. This relationship is reclaimed and fed by our practices of the faith—not for the sake of producing fruits in others, but for the rich harvest of life the Holy Spirit would produce in us.

This section is intended to help call us back to our first love. Again and again I've been called back to my own faith practices, usually after the business and "busy-ness" of my ministry have crowded them out of my daily life. I pray that these devotions will be a gift from one constantly renewing leader to others.

1 NO LONGER TOSSED ABOUT

Ephesians 4:7-16

My neighbor has a great lot on a point on Crystal Lake in Minnesota. Because the lot is so beautiful, he decided to remodel and expand his home there. After evaluating the initial estimates, he decided on a plan, and the remodeling began. It wasn't long before he discovered the first major difficulty: The foundation of his home was so cracked that building on it would compromise the integrity of the entire structure. For example, if the strong winds of a good Midwestern storm blew up, his home could literally collapse! Faced with this new information and the costs of repairing the foundation, he and his wife decided to tear the entire house down and build from a new foundation up. This was costly, and he and his family had to find provisional housing for a year as the old house was torn down and a new one was built.

The writer of the letter to the Ephesians (which tradition ascribes to Paul) wants Christ's church and its leaders to be built upon a solid foundation. See what care God has taken in building the church: "But to each one of us grace has been given as Christ apportioned it...It was he who gave some to be apostles, some to be prophets, some to be evangelists, and some to be pastors and teachers" (Ephesians 4:7, 11). The foundation for the church is God's grace in gifts given. Christian leaders understand that the ministry is gift-based by God's design. This is not a *possible* way of organizing Christ's church; this is the intent of God, the designer and builder of the church.

AS WE DISCOVER OUR GIFTS, WE LEARN OF OUR INADEQUACIES.

The personal discipleship of the leader is established in her or his awareness of these gifts. As we discover our gifts, we learn of our inadequacies. Clearly the text tells us that not all are apostles or pastors or evangelists. These are the particular foundation stones of Christ's church and are scattered among the believers. This means that our discipleship is a partnership with Christ and with others in the discovery and sharing of our particular gifts.

The writer is suggesting to us that effective leaders always build on the model of Christ's church. Effective leadership recognizes the leader's personal gifts as well as the need of the leader for the gift sets of others. A sure foundation is not built on the gifts of only one person, no matter how great those gifts may be, any more than a foundation consists of one stone by itself.

One of the great cracks in the foundation of many ministries is the leader's assumption that he or she must be all that is necessary. This perfectionism is a denial of the very basis of this remarkable passage: "But to each one of us *grace* has been given" (Ephesians 4:7). The tragedy of such perfectionism is burnout and isolation. Grace is given to those who are insufficient in and of themselves. God has designed the very foundation of our ministries to be both a celebration of our gifts and a clear understanding of our need for others.

A great leadership lesson from this text, then, is that effective leaders *celebrate their inadequacies*! In so doing, we acknowledge our reliance upon God's grace as well as God's design that ministry is always a team effort. We do not shoulder the responsibilities nor harvest the blessings alone. This is the joy of the church.

WE DO NOT SHOULDER THE RESPONSIBILITIES NOR HARVEST THE BLESSINGS ALONE. THIS IS THE JOY OF THE CHURCH.

The design of God's foundation has two expected outcomes, according to this text. The first is that others will be turned loose for ministry, "to prepare God's people for works of service, so that the body of Christ [the church] may be built up" (Ephesians 4:12).

A biblical foundation for Christian leadership leads to the discovery and sharing of the gifts of others *for ministry*. The design of God is that personal gifts always serve a greater purpose. Leaders understand that gifts that are claimed and used privately are misused. The consequence of such misuse is both the compromising of the strength of the body of Christ and the loss of purpose within the individual. Such private faith cracks the foundation of Christ's church. How often have we seen the squandering of great potential because gifted individuals have kept their gifts to themselves? Leaders are willing to call others to their gifts with the clear understanding that, in doing so, their lives will be blessed with the joy of purposive self-discovery. As we grow in sharing our giftedness, the church is blessed and grows. Leaders understand this marvelous dynamic in God's design.

The second outcome of God's foundation-building is very personal. We read, "Then we will no longer be infants, tossed back and forth by the waves, and blown here and there by every wind of teaching and by the cunning and craftiness of men in their deceitful scheming" (Ephesians 4:14).

The proof of a strong foundation is that when the winds blow, the house still stands. Christian leaders understand that our ministries are as strong as the spiritual foundation upon which we have built our lives. Personal discipleship provides that sturdy foundation. The writer of this passage knows that leaders will face the seductive powers of falsehood as well as the conflict and challenges created by "cunning and craftiness…[and] deceitful scheming."

This remarkable passage of Scripture suggests that our personal discipleship is the basis from which we will be able to withstand the difficulties all leaders face. Sooner or later every leader will be criticized, misunderstood, and misjudged. The only foundation strong enough is the grace of God in Jesus Christ. This same grace will not only withstand such challenges but also transform them into opportunities for our faith to grow. We read, "Instead, speaking the truth in love, we will in all things grow up into him who is the Head, that is, Christ" (Ephesians 4:15).

THE DESIGN OF GOD IS THAT PERSONAL GIFTS ALWAYS SERVE A GREATER PURPOSE.

This is the leadership promise in this text: God will present with every difficulty an opportunity to grow in faith and love—to grow into Christ. All that is required of us is that we are willing to learn. To hear and speak the truth in the love of Christ is to exercise such openness. As leaders rely upon God's grace and claim their gifts, they are provided a secure foundation from which to discern the truth and to know if that truth is said in the love of Christ. God's truth and the love of Christ tear down only in order to build up…just like my neighbor's deconstruction and reconstruction of his home.

The leader's practices of personal discipleship lay the foundation for effective ministry and faith. The leader's practices of personal discipleship nurture his or her willingness to be open to God's work in all things. The leader's practice of personal discipleship claims the leadership promise of this text.

LEADERSHIP PRAYER

Gracious God, thank you for the great truths of your Word. Build a sure foundation within me. Help me practice my discipleship of Jesus by trusting your grace and the gifts you have given me. Remind me to see the gifts you have given to others, and empower me to be more effective at helping them discover and share those gifts. But most of all, I ask you to nurture within me the necessary willingness to grow through all things—even the seasons of criticism and hardship that all leaders must endure. Help me remember that I am not alone in the tasks you have set before me. In Jesus' name, amen.

TEAM *Matters*

Objective: for leaders to begin to discover the importance of their own giftedness and to understand that their journey of discipleship is the foundation of their ministries.

Items needed: a gift bag for each participant, with ten to twelve "building items" in each bag.

Preparation: Before this session, gather six wooden building blocks for each participant. Write the following words on the blocks, one word or phrase per block: *prayer, worship, reading the Bible, serving, relating to others,* and *giving.* Place each set of blocks in a gift bag along with four to six other building items such as pieces of cardboard, Tinkertoys, LEGOS, and Lincoln Logs (make sure these items vary from bag to bag). Prepare a bag for each participant.

CHALLENGE Give each person a gift bag, but do not allow participants to open the bags until everyone has one and you have completed your instructions. Tell participants that they've each been given a gift and that they are each to build a house with that gift in the next three to five minutes. After answering questions, let them start building. As they build, some may be frustrated, while others may be interested in the fact that some things are similar in each bag and other things are different. Try not to answer any questions, but let the questions and comments fly. When the time is up, have each person share a bit about his or her house.

INTERACT Then ask participants to combine their "resources" to build a house together. Give them about five minutes. See how the energy changes in the room. When the time is up, encourage the group to discuss the experience.

READ & REFLECT Ask everyone to read Ephesians 4:7-16. Then encourage participants to reflect upon this Scripture and the activity by forming groups of two or three and discussing the questions on the following page. You may want them to discuss as many questions as time allows or select certain questions that you feel are especially relevant to your group. You may also give everyone a photocopy of the questions to facilitate discussion. ■

Getting REAL

- What gifts has God given you? How are you using those gifts to build up the body of Christ? How is your ministry encouraging others to use their gifts?

Think of one person whom you will encourage to use his or her gifts this week!

- On a scale of one to ten, rate the strength of your foundation right now (one—needs to be totally rebuilt; ten—God has done a great job!). What does your foundation need?

Commit to take action on this in the coming week. Ask another person to pray for you and hold you accountable.

- What "cunning" teachings or "crafty" schemes are testing your foundation? What's testing the foundation of your church or ministry? What are three things you can do to hold fast and not be "tossed back and forth"?

As a group, decide what one thing you will act on this week.

- "Speaking the truth in love" can be hard. Do you face any situations in which you need to do this? How can you meet this challenge? Share as much as you can with your partner, and take time right now to pray with him or her.
- "But to each one of us, grace has been given..." When has God's grace been especially evident in your life? How have you seen his grace in your ministry or in your church? Who do you know who needs to experience special grace today?

Commit to pray for that person each day this week.

2 STEADFAST IN FAITH
Colossians 1:21-23

He met me in the entryway of the church after worship. After a smile and greeting, his expression changed. "I'm not sure that I liked what you said about forgiveness today," he said. "Are you sure that, as a Christian, I am commanded to forgive others?"

"Yes," I replied, "that's what Jesus said. But I want to remind you that it is for our benefit that he commands us to forgive. It may not change the other person at all."

"Well, I just got an invitation to my niece's wedding. It came from the brother I haven't spoken to in fifteen years. I suppose I should go, shouldn't I?"

I encouraged him to go to the wedding, and three weeks later, he met me after church with a big smile. "My brother and I made up after fifteen years of silent resentment. If he hadn't sent that invitation, I never would have known he was even willing to see me—let alone make up and be real brothers again. That sermon was a real gift. And that was the best trip I ever made."

In this section of his letter to the Colossians, Paul invites us to see Jesus as God's invitation to a new relationship. The coming of Jesus—his life, ministry, death, and resurrection—serves as God's invitation to humanity to come and be reconciled. We read, "Once you were alienated from God and were enemies in your minds because of your evil behavior. But now he has reconciled you by Christ's physical body through death to present you holy in his sight, without blemish and free from accusation" (Colossians 1:21-22).

As Christian leaders, we understand that we have been invited into relationship with the Father, and this invitation has come entirely from God! Like my friend who did nothing to effect a reconciliation with his brother until he received that wedding invitation, we understand God's attitude toward us in a radical new way through Jesus Christ. His death makes us worthy. As he is unblemished and holy, so are we in God's eyes.

But the text doesn't stop there. Paul inserts a provisional clause: "if you continue in your faith, established and firm, not moved from the hope held out in the gospel. This is the gospel that you heard"(Colossians 1:23a).

The wedding invitation my friend received was simply that, an invitation. It couldn't change his life unless he acted upon it.

THE INVITATION TO GRACE IS EXTENDED TO US DAILY. AND DAILY WE NEED TO CLAIM IT.

He had to trust that it was genuine and then attend the wedding. The death and resurrection of Jesus are just such an invitation. For the invitation to change our lives, we must trust it and act upon it.

In this passage, Paul is not talking about coming to faith. He is speaking to people like you and me. He knows that the invitation to grace is extended to us daily. And daily we need to claim it.

As leaders, we are invited to enter a new way of thinking and living. This is a way of trusting God's love. One of the great enemies of this new way is our tendency toward perfectionism. Leaders usually expect more of themselves than anyone else does. This expectation can slide so easily into an internal demand that we be perfect.

If you are like me, you can receive one hundred compliments and one or two criticisms—and it's the criticisms you remember the most! We are constantly tempted to punish ourselves when we aren't universally praised. We think that if we could have done something differently, then we would have received no criticisms at all. So we hold ourselves accountable for what we could not have known. This doesn't mean that we shouldn't learn from healthy criticism. We ought not, however, punish ourselves with them! When we cannot let go of the two criticisms for the sake of the hundred affirmations, we are returning God's invitation unopened!

Our personal spiritual practice of discipleship includes clinging to the love of God in Jesus—a love that has nothing to do with our efforts! Being perfect, or close to it, has never been required. God does not require us to be what we cannot be, and neither should we. Daily Scripture reading and prayer, combined with weekly worship—not an expectation of perfection at every turn—will allow us to continue in our faith.

GOD DOES NOT REQUIRE US TO BE WHAT WE CANNOT BE, AND NEITHER SHOULD WE.

One of my personal mantras is this: *We cannot know what we don't know until we know it.* I know it sounds silly, but it reminds me how easy it is to punish myself with hindsight. I think, "If only I had seen that" or "Why didn't I see that?" Leaders are tempted to evaluate past actions and decisions based upon today's insights. But those insights weren't available then. Continuing in the faith means that we learn from the past but we don't punish ourselves for what we didn't know or see at the time.

Paul knew this. When lamenting his habit of doing what he wished he wouldn't and not doing what he wished he would have, he ends up where all Christian leaders eventually must—before the crucified Savior. Like Paul, we cry, "What a wretched man I am! Who will rescue me from this body of death? Thanks be to God—through Jesus Christ our Lord!" (Romans 7:24-25a). Only God's great invitation to enter into a relationship with him can set us free for a life worth living. This is the gift that Paul wanted the Colossian Christians—and you and me—to live in. And this is how we, as leaders, continue to be anchored in "the hope held out in the gospel" (Colossians 1:23b).

As Christian leaders we need to be reminded of this wonderful grace through the practice of forgiving ourselves in Jesus' name. Living in the gospel frees us to learn from our mistakes and failures without being imprisoned by them through our own guilt. Jesus has taken our guilt on the cross, including the guilt that stems from the knowledge of our inadequacies.

I invite you to join me in practicing self-forgiveness—in Jesus' name. Then, as a leader, share this aspect of personal discipleship with others.

LEADERSHIP PRAYER

Gracious God, you have invited me to be reconciled with you. I confess that I sometimes live as if that has nothing to do with how I treat myself. As I practice my faith, help me to live in your forgiveness by forgiving myself. I want to act upon your wonderful invitation to come near to you. As I work with others, help me to encourage us to learn from our mistakes and failures without allowing them to imprison us. Let your hope be planted again within me. Amen.

TEAM *Matters*

Objective: to invite participants to forgive themselves and to challenge them to forgive others.

Items needed: a white board, a dry-erase marker and eraser, a blank sheet of paper for each participant, note cards and envelopes, pens, matches, and a metal trash can.

Preparation: Before the session, write the following message on note cards, one note card for each participant: "You are mine! I love you, and nothing you do will change that. Today I want to start fresh with our relationship, wiping away any issues that stand between us. Love, God." Place these notes in envelopes, and seal them. In addition, gather enough blank note cards and envelopes for everyone to receive one. Do not seal the envelopes containing the blank cards.

CHALLENGE Standing by the white board, welcome the group and invite everyone to join in a reflection exercise. Write these words at the top of the board: *difficulty, consequences,* and *current status*. Ask participants to consider your shared ministry's

TEAM *Matters*

(continued)

history and identify five times that were especially difficult. Perhaps it was an internal leadership issue or an external event that affected the ministry. Maybe it was a financial issue that divided the congregation or a power struggle among ministry teams. As participants identify those events, list them in the column marked *difficulty*. Then ask members of the team to reflect on the consequences for the ministry of each issue. Finally, ask participants to describe the current status of each issue. Allow as much time as you think necessary. (It's not necessary to address all the issues.) Then read 1 John 1:8-9, and erase everything on the white board, telling the group that all of these issues are over, erased, forgiven. Encourage the team to receive God's grace, to recognize that God has moved beyond these mistakes, and to move beyond them as well.

APPLY Use the next part of the activity to invite participants to embrace, on a personal level, the grace given to them. Give everyone a blank sheet of paper and a pen. Ask participants to write these words—*mistakes*, *consequences*, and *current status*—at the top of the page. Then ask them to list five situations or mistakes that are blocking them from living as God would have them live. Finally, ask them to describe, in writing, the consequences and current status of each. Give participants five to ten minutes to do this.

When participants have finished, have them fold their papers and take them to the front of the room. As they watch, burn the papers. Hand everyone two note cards, one with the message you wrote earlier and one blank card. Have participants return to their seats and read the card with the message. Then ask them each to write a note to someone they know who might need to hear about God's grace today.

READ & REFLECT Ask everyone to read Colossians 1:21-23. Then encourage participants to reflect upon this Scripture and the activity by forming groups of two or three and discussing the questions on the following page. You may want them to discuss as many questions as time allows or select certain questions that you feel are especially relevant to your group. You may also give everyone a photocopy of the questions to facilitate discussion. ■

Getting REAL

• How would you describe the experience of watching your sins "disappear"? What thoughts went through your mind? How have your sins kept you from living in God's grace? Have you let situations from your past keep you from sharing God's love?

Place the card you received today in your bathroom mirror. Begin and end each day by remembering God's love for you.

• How often do you need to be reminded of your fresh start with Jesus Christ? What influences make it hard to remember this? What experiences from your past distract you from living in God's grace?

Write the words of Colossians 1:21-23 on a slip of paper and carry it with you this week. Each time the sins of your past begin to haunt you, read these words.

• The Bible talks a lot about forgiveness. Share your favorite scriptural story or verse about forgiveness. Or read some of the following Scriptures and share what they mean to you with regard to forgiveness: Matthew 5:23-24; Matthew 18:15-20; Matthew 18:21-22; Luke 7:36-50; and Luke 15:11-31.

Practice handing your sins over to God by writing down your sins at the end of each day and burning them. As they burn, say a prayer of thanksgiving.

3 NO LONGER ANXIOUS
Philippians 4:4-7

I wasn't sure how she would react. Our friends Mark and Sue had come to see our new grandson and say hello to our twenty-two-month-old granddaughter, Emme. Emme, usually an outgoing toddler, had just entered her shy stage. Now Mark wanted to play with her. She ducked her head into her grandmother's neck as Mark gently called to her and invited her to play.

Emme glanced up at her grandmother, then across to her mother, and, seeing that they were near and not anxious, she turned to Mark and smiled. In short order these two were laughing and playing. Her shyness lost, Emme and Mark became great and joyous friends that evening.

I don't know about you, but the Bible's insistence that we, as Christians, do not worry about anything has seemed to me to be unrealistic, at the very least. The human condition brings with it a natural inclination toward anxiety. We have all heard of the "flight or fight" mechanism that is a part of human nature. When we perceive that we are threatened, this anxiety response naturally kicks in. First our hearts beat more rapidly; then we breathe more quickly and shallowly as adrenaline courses through our bodies. And we seem incapable of changing that. How can we let go of anxiety and worry when they are so natural...so biological?

In this section of Paul's letter to the Philippians, we are instructed to do two seemingly impossible things. First, Paul tells us, "Rejoice in the Lord always. I will say it again: Rejoice!" (Philippians 4:4). How does that work? I can't control my feelings. Sometimes I am sad and down. Sometimes anxiety clasps my heart, and I become timid or shy in the face of life. It seems impossible to rejoice in all circumstances. But that is what Paul is telling us to do.

Second, we read: "Do not be anxious about anything" (Philippians 4:6a). Right. When the job turns sour and the boss is more demanding than ever, when there is too much month at the end of the paycheck, or when my relationship with my spouse or child or best friend is on the rocks, I am supposed to face it with serenity.

In the face of such passages of the Bible, many people have a hard time accepting faith as relevant or even attainable. In fact, Christian leaders struggle with the same issues.

But I learned something from Emme that evening. Her anxiety was relieved, but not because anything external had changed. Mark was still a new person to her. Her grandmother and her mother hadn't changed where they sat or how they were behaving. Her attitude changed when she realized that both her mother and her grandmother *were near to her.* Her understanding of their closeness changed everything!

IT SEEMS IMPOSSIBLE TO REJOICE IN ALL CIRCUMSTANCES. BUT THAT IS WHAT PAUL IS TELLING US TO DO.

In this passage Paul reminds us that these two seemingly impossible requirements of faith become possible only in the presence of Jesus. The instruction to rejoice in the Lord always leads into the verse in which we are called to be free from anxiety. The heart of this section is Philippians 4:5b: "The Lord is near." Joy is increased and anxiety reduced when we are reminded that we do not face any situation alone—the Lord is near! No matter how overwhelming the circumstances, we can "in everything, by prayer and petition, with thanksgiving, present [our] requests to God" (Philippians 4:6b). The Lord is near, so we can be bold in our prayers! This boldness is the antidote to anxiety. When we become shy before life, we need to look up and see the Savior…just as my granddaughter looked up and saw that her mother was near.

The promise of this text is in its final verse: "And the peace of God, which transcends all understanding, will guard your hearts and your minds in Christ Jesus" (Philippians 4:7). Notice how this promise is tied to the nearness of the Savior. It is *in Christ Jesus* that we find this peace.

The leadership lesson here is that God's serenity is a gift. We read that it is beyond our understanding. We can't figure it out. But when it comes, it comes through the felt nearness of Jesus—just as Emme's openness to Mark's friendship was a gift resulting from the nearness of her grandmother and mother.

How can we experience the nearness of God? Is there a way for leaders to grow in our awareness of the Savior's presence? The text suggests two ways of getting in touch with Jesus' presence in our lives. The first is found in the words "Let your gentleness be evident to all" (Philippians 4:5a). In the ancient church, Christians were taught that all of life was lived *coram dei*—before God. So how they related to their families, to those in authority, or even to those they met in the streets, was a living testimony that they brought the presence of God there.

In our day, the question most frequently asked of Christians by those who are inquiring about faith is "What difference does Jesus make in your daily life?" Leaders understand that we experience and reflect the nearness of Christ when we can call upon his grace in any moment of our lives.

At Prince of Peace, we have given members of our congregation green dots and asked them to place the dots on their watches. Whenever they check the time, the dots remind them that it is always time to pray. I've been told that people who have felt angry have looked at their watches and, seeing that green dot, changed their attitudes. A friend has his green dot on his car's rearview mirror. Whenever he is cut off in traffic, it reminds him to pray instead of say all those things he used to say. A green dot can serve as a reminder of Jesus' nearness.

Leaders understand the need for such practices. Because he has discovered the power of the green dot to change his attitude and behavior while driving, my friend has begun "green-dotting" others. Whenever he has a chance, he shares a green dot with others...along with an explanation of its meaning.

Paul also tells us that we experience the presence of God when we are eager to pray. We read, "in everything, by prayer and petition, with thanksgiving, present your requests to God" (Philippians 4:6b).

Personal discipleship is a life of prayer. Leaders understand the power of time with Jesus Christ through prayer. Prayer invites us into the presence of God. Only in God's presence can we find joy and peace. If rejoicing and anxiety-free living were possible without prayer, Paul would hardly have taken the time to encourage us to pray. If we were constantly aware of Jesus' presence, then Paul would not have spoken so frequently of our need to seek it.

God's nearness through the power of the Holy Spirit is like the air we breathe. We don't think of the air until we suddenly find it in short supply—on a long run or after a sudden exertion, for example. But it is always there. Prayer simply brings to our conscious mind what we already know is there.

I find it a great affirmation of the truth of this Scripture that people instinctively pray in times of difficulty. God has planted within every human heart the need to feel his presence. When we find ourselves in over our heads, we naturally turn to God. The promise of this passage of Philippians is that God will hear our prayers. Christian leaders can confidently point to Paul's language and show that he gives no instructions on how we ought to pray or express our petitions. Nor does Paul tell us that certain petitions are too big or too small for our Savior. He simply says to confidently go to the One who is already near and trust him with whatever is on our hearts and minds. There is no prayer too small nor any petition too great that God will not hear it.

PRAYER SIMPLY BRINGS TO OUR CONSCIOUS MIND WHAT WE ALREADY KNOW IS THERE.

Now that's cause to rejoice! Jesus invites us to a real relationship. We can share whatever is before us with the One who is already in it. And in our sharing, we are blessed by his presence. We know we are loved. We can trust that we are heard and that, in the wisdom of eternity, God will respond. And we can receive the peace of God. We can breathe more easily because we are surrounded by an abundance of what we need.

Isn't it true that Christians often act from a "scarcity theology"? We tend to live our hours and days as if there is a scarcity of grace! We seem to think that only when we ask the right thing in the right way will we receive a dollop of God's provision. Paul, beleaguered and imprisoned, knew and celebrated the abundance of God! If any situation was dire and worthy of high anxiety, it was Paul's. But it was precisely in that situation that he called us to rejoice in the presence of the Lord. And, although nothing about Paul's external circumstances changed, everything else changed. God took even Paul's imprisonment and made of it a great witness.

Have you experienced the abundant presence of Jesus Christ in a time of need? If you have, then you know how your circumstances may not have immediately changed but, inside yourself, everything was different. Christian leaders who experience God's presence know that the abundance of God is found in who God is, not in what is happening around them or to them.

LEADERSHIP PRAYER

Lord Jesus, I simply want to acknowledge that you are as near to me in this moment as the air I breathe. Thank you for your faithfulness. Remind me, whenever I am anxious or unable to experience joy, that you are with me. Restore my heart. Grow my faith as I practice prayer and gentleness with others. Amen.

TEAM *Matters*

Objective: for leaders to discover God's peace and experience that peace every day, even in anxious times.

Items needed: note cards, a pen for each person, a CD player, and the song "Draw Me Close" by Kelly Carpenter, which may be found on Michael W. Smith's *Worship* CD.

READ & INTERACT Begin by reading aloud Philippians 4:4-7. Then ask participants to listen for a key phrase that resonates with them as you read the passage a second time. After the second reading, have participants share their phrases with the group. Form six groups, and assign each a key word or phrase from the passage: *rejoice, anxious, gentleness, the Lord is near, peace,* or *prayer.* Distribute photocopies of the reflection questions (pp. 24-25), and ask the groups to discuss the questions associated with the words or phrases assigned to them. (The groups should be fairly small. If there are more than three people in a group, form another group.)

REFLECT As the groups conclude their discussions, gather everyone for a brief quiet time as you play "Draw Me Close" by Kelly Carpenter on a CD player. ■

Getting REAL

Rejoice—One dictionary defines *rejoice* as "to give joy to" or "to feel joy or great delight." When was the last time you truly rejoiced? Rejoicing is not something our society promotes, yet Philippians 4:4 says, "Rejoice in the Lord always. I will say it again: Rejoice!" Why would we be instructed, as Christians, to rejoice? Why is it so hard to rejoice in our world? What do we have to rejoice about? What things cause you to rejoice?

Practice rejoicing this week. Put yourself into a joyful mood or situations that lead you to truly rejoice.

Anxious—Remember a time you were anxious. What were the circumstances? What caused the anxiety? What were you feeling at the time, physically and emotionally? How did you shed your anxiety? Listen to the stories of the others in your group, and identify common feelings or experiences.

Gentleness—Would you be described as a gentle person? What do you think about this verse: "Let your gentleness be evident to all. The Lord is near." (Philippians 4:5)? Why would the Bible challenge us to be gentle? What is the relationship of gentleness to anxiety? In your group, list ten ways to practice gentleness. Write them on a note card, and place that card in your calendar or planner.

The Lord Is Near—Tell the members of your group about a time you could honestly say, "The Lord is near." What were the circumstances? (Were you alone or with others? Were you in church or on a mountaintop? Was it at the end of a week of camp or in Sunday morning worship? What else was going on in your life at the time? What external factors contributed to your sensing of God's presence? What internal factors contributed?) Describe your feelings. How would you tell someone how you knew God was with you at that time in your life?

Peace—Do you know the peace described in Philippians 4:7? Do you desire such peace? If so, do you seek it? Have you experienced it at some point in your life? If not, why not? Do you believe such peace is attainable? What is the promise that comes with knowing such peace?

→

Getting REAL

(continued)

Begin and end each day this week by reciting Philippians 4:7. Each day, write down how this kind of peace would affect your life. After seven days, review your notes and reflect on them.

Prayer—"But in everything, by prayer and petition, with thanksgiving, present your requests to God" (Philippians 4:6b). Evaluate your prayer life. Do you talk with God about your financial concerns? about family matters? about the health issue you are worried about? What about the stock market or the repairs needed on the car? If so, what happens after you share your concerns with God? If not, why not? Do you take your requests to God with a thankful heart? Make a list of the requests you have right now. Take a moment to give them over to God in a short prayer. Then exchange your list with another person in your group.

Pray for the things on each other's list in the coming week. The next time you meet, check in to see what happened!

4 THE RIGHT MIND-SET

Romans 8:5-11

A New York Times article printed on July 10, 2002, records a remarkable discovery. A visiting museum director from Scotland sifted through old boxes of drawings of light fixtures at the Cooper-Hewitt, National Design Museum in New York and uncovered what several experts agree is a work by Michelangelo.

The most remarkable aspect of this discovery is not that it is a Michelangelo but that, for decades, it existed under the very noses of art experts in a city that considers itself the capital of the art world. How is it possible that countless experts viewed the drawing—a large, intricate drawing in black chalk on cream-colored paper, seventeen inches high and ten inches wide—and never recognized the work of one of history's greatest and best known artists?

Perhaps it's because the drawing was purchased in 1942 for $60. The dealer who sold it to the museum considered it the work of an anonymous sixteenth-century Italian artist, so those who looked at it *saw it as such.* The mind-set of those countless art experts who viewed the work over the years predetermined that they would dismiss it.

On the other hand, Sir Timothy Clifford, the art expert who discovered the work, has a reputation as a "truffle hound" for art. Clifford's mind-set is to see a work for what it is, not to see it for what others think it is.

In Romans 8:5-11, Paul invites us to get the right mind-set. In verse 5 he says that "those who live according to the sinful nature have their *minds set* on what that nature desires; but those who live in accordance with the Spirit have their *minds set* on what the Spirit desires." And in verses 6 and 7a, he uses the word *mind* three times: "The mind of sinful man is death, but the mind controlled by the Spirit is life and peace; the sinful mind is hostile to God." In other words, what you see is determined by what your mind is set upon.

WHAT YOU SEE IS DETERMINED BY WHAT YOUR MIND IS SET UPON.

The personal practice of discipleship to which leaders are called is nothing less than nurturing the mind-set of faith. If we practice prayer and Scripture reading, for example, we will see God active in our world in ways that those who don't cannot. When we are willing to trust God's activity in our lives, we can submit to God's will and, by the power of the Holy Spirit, strive to do it. Without the mind-set of faith, there is no ability to *see*, let alone *do*, the will of God.

That's why Paul, the master artist of grace, proceeds to say, "Those controlled by the sinful nature cannot please God" (Romans 8:8). When our minds are set on what we want, what we believe is best for ourselves, we close ourselves off to the mind of the Spirit. We cannot know God's will. How can we then do it?

The Christian leader practices spiritual discipleship as the discipline of seeking the right mind-set—the mind-set of the Spirit of the living God. This is done both privately and, at times, publicly. Privately, we take the time to consciously enter God's presence and learn from the Holy Spirit. But, publicly, we seek the mind-set of faith as well. There are three ways leaders can publicly develop the mind-set of the Spirit.

First, whenever leaders find themselves at an impasse in a meeting or in making a decision, we can stop and truly seek the leading of God. Not long ago, as I was engaged with our board in a difficult conversation about a staff member, it became clear that we were stuck. We knew a decision had to be made, but we weren't certain of the right decision. That was when we stopped our conversation and publicly prayed. We asked for the Spirit's guidance and then were quiet for a few minutes. Afterward, the board reached a unanimous decision. Such moments of prayer may not always lead to this kind of certainty. There have been times we've publicly sought the mind-set of faith and still couldn't reach a decision. Trusting the God of the process, we have delayed making any decision.

WE STOPPED OUR CONVERSATION AND PUBLICLY PRAYED.

Second, leaders can practice the mind-set of faith in Christian service. When we are willing to give our time and energy in service to others, we are planting the mind-set of our servant Savior deeply within our souls. When serving Thanksgiving meals with the Salvation Army, my wife and I experienced the joy of meeting Christ in those we served. Adults and children clasped our hands and said, "Thank you." Many made a point of saying goodbye when they were leaving. The world suggests that these are graceless individuals who deserve the situations in which they find themselves. But we perceived that group very differently, and the mind-set of God, who values all people eternally, was reinforced within us.

Finally, leaders seek the mind-set of the Spirit when we are willing to publicly challenge the world's assumptions. This can be done obviously or discreetly. I watched as one of my pastoral colleagues quietly challenged our world's standards of beauty and value during a children's sermon not long ago.

Many children at Prince of Peace have disabilities. Some are confined to wheelchairs; others struggle to walk or talk. One Sunday morning, I watched as Pastor Paul invited the children forward. When one child was wheeled up and off to the side of the rest of the kids, Paul simply and naturally went to the child and, still talking to all the children, wheeled him closer and into the midst of the other kids.

Then, without any self-consciousness, he simply stroked the child's hair as if to say, "You are recognized and loved just as you are. You belong here, and you are handsome and worthy of eternity." That was the real children's sermon for me that day. It challenged me to be attentive in a way that I wished I had been but knew I hadn't.

I OFTEN WONDER IF, WHEN I STAND BEFORE THE THRONE OF GOD AND REVIEW MY LIFE, I'LL SEE ALL THE OPPORTUNITIES TO REFLECT JESUS THAT I MISSED.

The mind-set of the Spirit opens us to see such opportunities for active love, doesn't it? I often wonder if, when I stand before the throne of God and review my life, I'll see all the opportunities to reflect Jesus that I missed. Surely that would be even more painful than seeing my sins and shortcomings. Those missed opportunities stem from a failure to have the mind-set of the Spirit.

How many blessings will we bypass today because our minds are not set on the wonder of God's work in our lives and in our world? Today can we have the mind-set of the Spirit of which Paul writes? If so, we are promised that, no matter what happens, God will give us an abundance of real life. That's the promise in Romans 8:11: "And if the Spirit of him who raised Jesus from the dead is living in you, he who raised Christ from the dead will also give life to your mortal bodies through his Spirit, who lives in you." Surely this is not just a promise of eternal life but also of a vibrant spiritual life of joy and discovery today.

LEADERSHIP PRAYER

Today, O Lord, I pray that you will give me the right mind-set. I want to see with the Spirit's eyes and live by the Spirit's desires. Please help me to see the blessings you set before me today. If I can seek the mind-set of faith in any active way, just show me. I don't want to overlook one of your masterpieces because my mind-set is wrong. Increase your joy and purpose in my life by the leading of your Spirit, I pray. Amen.

TEAM *Matters*

Objective: to help leaders contrast sinful viewpoints with God's viewpoint.

Items needed: a photocopy of the Responsive Reading (p. 30) for everyone; index cards; a pen; a picture of Jesus on the cross; and four pictures of various things—perhaps one of nature, one of people, one of an object, and one of an event.

Preparation: Before this session, create two sets of cards. On one set of cards, write, "You see the world through God's eyes. You see love, joy, peace, patience, compassion, goodness, faithfulness, gentleness, and life." On the other set of cards, write, "You see the world through the eyes of sin. You see selfishness, pride, jealousy, hate, greed, anger, war, and death." Make enough "mind-set of the Spirit" cards for everyone and enough "sinful mind-set" cards for half of the group.

CHALLENGE Form two groups. Give everyone in Group 1 a "mind-set of the Spirit" card. Give everyone in Group 2 a "sinful mind-set" card. Explain that you will show everyone five pictures and that you will allow groups thirty seconds to view each picture with the particular perspective written on the cards they were given. After you show each picture, ask volunteers from each group to describe how they viewed it, based on the perspectives written on their cards.

For example, the first picture might portray a waterfall in a wooded setting. Someone in Group 1 might describe the scene as the home of hundreds of deer and other wildlife or a place people hike to each year to find spiritual and emotional replenishment. Someone in Group 2 might say that in a few short weeks the trees will be burned to the ground in a fire that will also kill wildlife and injure several firefighters.

READ Repeat this process with the other pictures, ending with the picture of Jesus on the cross. Distribute the photocopies of the Responsive Reading on page 30, and ask the groups to read aloud the sections of Romans 8:5-11 assigned to them. Complete the reading with the section assigned to the leader.

REFLECT After the reading, collect the "sinful mind-set" cards, and replace them with "mind-set of the Spirit" cards. Invite participants to see the world this week through God's eyes! If time allows, encourage participants to reflect upon the Scripture and the activity by forming groups of two or three and discussing the questions on page 31. ■

Responsive READING

ROMANS 8:5-11

Group 2: "Those who live according to the sinful nature have their minds set on what that nature desires;

Group 1: but those who live in accordance with the Spirit have their minds set on what the Spirit desires.

Group 2: The mind of sinful man is death,

Group 1: but the mind controlled by the Spirit is life and peace;

Group 2: the sinful mind is hostile to God. It does not submit to God's law, nor can it do so. Those controlled by the sinful nature cannot please God.

Group 1: You, however, are controlled not by the sinful nature but by the Spirit, if the Spirit of God lives in you.

Group 2: And if anyone does not have the Spirit of Christ, he does not belong to Christ.

Group 1: But if Christ is in you, your body is dead because of sin, yet your spirit is alive because of righteousness. And if the Spirit of him who raised Jesus from the dead is living in you, he who raised Christ from the dead will also give life to your mortal bodies through his Spirit, who lives in you."

Leader: "You see, at just the right time, when we were still powerless, Christ died for the ungodly...God demonstrates his own love for us in this: While we were still sinners, Christ died for us" (Romans 5:6, 8).

Getting REAL

- How did you respond to the contrasting viewpoints of the same pictures?

- What is your natural tendency: to view things through God's eyes or the eyes of the sinful nature? How does that affect your daily choices? What prevents you from seeing with God's eyes? What can you do to remove those barriers?

- A leader's perspective is always public. Who are some people who consistently model the mind-set of the Spirit in public?

What can you do to ensure that your mind-set reflects the Spirit, both publicly and privately? Write one or two actions on the back of your "mind-set of the Spirit" card, and place it in your car or office as a reminder to model publicly God's view of the world this week.

5 THE POWER OF OBEDIENCE

Luke 2:39-52

I can't remember the first time I went to church. One of my earliest memories was of our family worshipping in a school cafeteria. Part of a mission congregation, we sat on hard chairs before a small moveable altar and a piano. The pastor wore a suit and tie under his vestments. I recall that the singing was strong, the mood somber—until after the service. Then everyone got together and filled the room with conversation and laughter.

I also remember my parents' clear instructions that my three brothers and I were to be on our best behavior in church. The worst punishment was to be removed from the service for a reprimand. But the more usual punishment was administered by my father as his long arm reached across anyone sitting between us and squeezed my leg just below the knee. This was so dreaded that my brothers and I would often jockey for position to ensure we'd be farthest from Dad. It didn't matter. Dad had the longest arms of any man I ever knew.

What we didn't understand was that we were being prepared for a life of worship. The practice of obedience and the idea that faithful Christians gather weekly to come before God were set deeply within all of us. More than any lecture or confirmation, Sunday school or youth ministry lesson, my parents set the example for coming before God.

Jesus must have had, beyond his divine essence, just this kind of modeling. In our text, we see how the faithful earthly parents of Jesus were obedient to the worship laws as they understood them—just as mine were.

Most Christians are familiar with the story of Jesus astonishing the teachers in the Temple in Jerusalem. But note how Luke sets the stage. We read in Luke 2:39: "When Joseph and Mary had done everything required by the Law of the Lord…" Again, in Luke 2:41, we find the theme of parental modeling of faith through obedience: "Every year his parents went to Jerusalem for the Feast of the Passover." Joseph and Mary were chosen by God to be the earthly parents of Jesus because their faith was a natural part of their lives. They not only did what was required, but they also fulfilled the greater good by making an annual pilgrimage to Jerusalem for Passover. Surely this was not lost on the developing boy, Jesus.

After leaving Jerusalem, Mary and Joseph assumed that members of their extended family were watching Jesus, but they weren't. After realizing he was absent, they frantically searched for their son, and when they finally found him, they did what every parent since Adam and Eve has done: They responded out of their anxiety. His mother said to him, "Son, why have you treated us like this? Your father and I have been anxiously searching for you" (Luke 2:48b). In other words, she interpreted his behavior as an act of rebellion against her and his father. Jesus simply responded that his actions had little to do with them and everything to do with his relationship with his heavenly Father.

If you are like me, it is easy to personalize behavior that has caused us anxiety or pain. When someone chooses to leave the congregation or our ministry, it is natural to assume that the departure is a judgment about us. When a criticism is voiced, no matter how reasonable, most of us feel bad. But as Christian leaders, it is important for us to learn to differentiate issues from persons. Jesus stayed in Jerusalem to "be in his Father's house," not to cause his earthly parents anxiety. Sometimes people's decisions have unintended repercussions on others. I believe that Mary and Joseph began to understand this spiritual truth in a profound way after this experience.

IT IS IMPORTANT FOR US TO LEARN TO DIFFERENTIATE ISSUES FROM PERSONS.

That brings us back to the lesson of modeling our discipleship before others—especially our children. The lesson wasn't lost on our Lord. Luke confirmed this when he wrote, "Then he [Jesus] went down to Nazareth with them and *was obedient to them*" (Luke 2:51). The power of their obedience was reflected in that of Jesus—not just to God the Father, but to Mary and Joseph as his earthly parents. Our obedience has the power to instill obedience in the lives of others, especially those closest to us.

Mary and Joseph weren't obedient to the law of God because they wanted Jesus to learn obedience. It was natural to them. My father and mother worshipped, not to develop worshipful spirits in their children but because worship was a natural extension of their faith. The power of obedience is set loose when we obey for the right reason. The right reason for obedience is our desire to be faithful to our faithful God. When we do that, we can only imagine the Spirit's power to multiply the good stemming from our obedience.

I have never spoken to my father about this memory I've shared with you. I suspect he would be surprised. But I have received the blessings of his and my mother's obedience. Jesus did too. This chapter in Luke's Gospel ends by describing the blessings God multiplied in our Lord through his obedience: "And Jesus grew in wisdom and stature, and in favor with God and men" (Luke 2:52).

I believe that our heartfelt obedience to the will of God has the potential to produce similar results in those we love. Can a parent or grandparent pray for a greater blessing in the life of a child? Can a spouse or friend pray for a greater blessing in the lives of others? I don't believe so. Our willingness to obey God is a treasure that God will set before others. Personal discipleship sets loose the power of obedience in our lives as well as in the lives of others.

LEADERSHIP PRAYER

Lord Jesus, as you were obedient to your earthly parents as well as your heavenly Father, I ask that you would nurture in me a willingness to obey you. Grow in my heart the desire and will to follow you. Then help me trust that my obedience will be a witness to unlock blessings in the lives of others. Amen.

TEAM *Matters*

Objective: for leaders to discover the private and public impact of obedience on their discipleship walk.

Items needed: a sheet of 11x17-inch paper for each participant and a handful of colored pencils or markers.

CHALLENGE Help participants make timelines of their lives. Tell them to make a dot on the left side of the paper to mark the day they were born. Tell them to make a dot on the right side to mark today. Then tell them to connect the two with a line that represents God's presence with them in their journey so far.

Next have participants draw a second line, using a different color of pencil or marker. This line represents their distance from God at various points in their lives. (For example, perhaps one participant grew up in a Christian home and was active in the church. The second line would closely parallel the first line for this part of her life. Then she went to college and departed from the faith practices of her youth; at this point the second line would diverge sharply from the first. Just before she married, she began to reconnect with God, so the second line might merge with the first, and so on.) Once participants have finished, ask them each to share their timelines with another person.

READ & REFLECT Finally, ask everyone to read Luke 2:39-52 and form groups of two or three to discuss the questions on the following page. (You may want them to discuss as many questions as time allows or select certain questions that you feel are especially relevant to your group.) ■

Getting REAL

1. Name some people you looked up to when you were a child.
- What about those people caused you to look up to them?
- Who are some people you look up to now? Why?
- How has the very fact that you have people to look up to influenced your life?

This week, pray for the people who have touched your life.

2. When you were a child, did you ever wander away from your parents?
- What caught your attention or caused you to wander off?
- If you were to "wander off" today, what do you think would be the cause?
- If you had three days of discovery, as Jesus did, what would you do with that time?
- How did Jesus' time in the Temple augment his commitment to obedience?
- Do you think your discovery time would augment your obedience to God? If so, how?

Take time each of the next three days to reflect on what God is asking of you right now. Write your reflections in a journal.

3. Review Luke 2:39-52. Which person in this story do you most closely resemble? Why?
- Would your response be the same as or different from that person's?
- When you hear the word *obedience*, what is the first thing that comes to mind?
- Is that response reflected in your character?

In the days ahead, pay attention to your behavior. Does it reflect the character of the person in the story?

4. Who watches your behavior? Your kids or other family members? Co-workers? People in your congregation? People at the grocery store?
- What does your behavior reveal about your faith?
- Are you willing to be bolder in publicly demonstrating your discipleship journey?
- What would you want others to learn from watching you?
- What can you do to point people to Christ?

Choose four things to add to or change about your life. Focus on living out one of them each of the next four weeks.

6 PERSISTENT PRAYER
Luke 18:1-8

"How's your prayer life, Pastor Mike?" Joe asked with a grin. He met me in the church parking lot after worship. In the sermon I had encouraged the congregation to be a discipleship community that dares to care about one another's spiritual life and, in keeping with that theme, had suggested that they could ask me about mine. Joe was taking me at my word.

Without thinking, I simply replied, "Just fine, Joe."

And, with a smile and "Have a great day, Pastor Mike," Joe turned and began to walk away.

IT SEEMED THAT MY PRAYERS WERE GOING UP BUT NOTHING WAS COMING DOWN.

As I turned, it occurred to me that I had just lied. My prayer life wasn't so hot. There was conflict among some of our leadership at the church, a member of my extended family with whom I was very close was in the midst of a divorce, and I was burdened by some friends' serious medical problems. I was in a spiritual desert. I continued to pray, but it seemed that my prayers were going up but nothing was coming down. All I heard from God was silence.

With a sigh of resignation, I turned and called out, "Joe." He turned, and we walked toward each other. "I'm sorry, Joe. That isn't the truth. The fact is that my prayer life is really hard right now. I just can't seem to hear the voice of God."

Joe's jaw dropped—he really hadn't expected this answer from his senior pastor! Then he smiled kindly and said, "Pastor Mike, I'll pray for you. I know it will get better. God will speak to you. Sometimes it just takes time."

Christian leaders know the power of prayer. We have seen its effects in the lives of others. We have experienced it in our own lives. But, as Luke 18:1-8 reminds us, we also know that there are times God seems distant and silent and that it is in those times that prayer is a discipline. The call of our Lord in this text is twofold.

First, recognize that it is natural to experience seasons of praying with no apparent response from God. Luke introduces this teaching of Jesus with this instruction in mind: "Then Jesus told his disciples a parable to show them that they should always pray *and not give up*" (Luke 18:1). Sometimes Christian leaders are tempted to give up on prayer. I was in just such a circumstance when Joe and I spoke. Like any other relationship, our relationship with Jesus Christ can be disturbed, interrupted, and confused by circumstances. Just as we can drive out of the range of a radio station's signal, so can the static of our personal situations drown out the voice of God.

What a gift God has given us in the community of faith! Joe personified Luke for me. His words had the effect of Luke's retelling of Jesus' teaching. Joe's faith witnessed to my faith. I no longer felt alone in that desert. At least one other person would be praying specifically for me.

The hardest part for leaders, of course, is to be willing to tell the truth and let others in. I knew Joe. I knew I could trust him. I also knew that my own integrity was on the line. Both of these elements came into play when I turned and got past the standard clergy reply. I know that if I had been asked by someone I didn't know, or perhaps couldn't trust, my response might have been less truthful and very different. But God sent someone who could hear what I needed to say.

Leadership is a vulnerable place to serve our Lord, isn't it? We can feel isolated and, because of our sense of responsibility to others, withdraw even from those who would support us when we are troubled. I believe that is why Christian leaders are always called to serve within a community. God will provide some people with whom we can be real and still lead. The risk for such sharing clearly needs to be set within the boundaries of spiritual discernment. But sooner or later, leaders will be in situations in which our own need for the support of the community is obvious.

GOD WILL PROVIDE SOME PEOPLE WITH WHOM WE CAN BE REAL AND STILL LEAD.

The second teaching of our Lord follows up on the first: Prayer is to be persistent. Our personal discipleship is not dependent upon always receiving or hearing the direction of God's Spirit. We pray—and continue to pray—out of obedience to this command of Christ. That is when God's promise meets our obedience. "And the Lord said, 'Listen to what the unjust judge says. And will not God bring about justice for his chosen ones, who cry out to him day and night? Will he keep putting them off? I tell you, he will see that they get justice, and quickly' " (Luke 18:6-8a).

I am struck by the questions Jesus asks us to consider. The first question presumes that there has been a time of intense praying, "day and night." This suggests that the prayers have been going on for some time without a discernible answer. The second question suggests the same thing. Jesus asks if we really believe that our God will put off answering our prayers indefinitely. The point is that there will be times such questions will naturally arise in the heart and soul of a Christian leader. Jesus wants us not to be put off by such doubts but to see in his sensitive teaching the promise that God will hear and respond to our persistent prayers. God will act. And when God acts for justice—to make the wrong right and exercise redemption to buy back our joy in life—God will act in a swift and sure manner.

That's what Joe spoke to me about. God will hear. Keep on praying. Know that you are not praying alone. It may be awhile, but God will surely answer.

And, by the way, God did.

LEADERSHIP PRAYER

O Lord Jesus, thank you for understanding me and loving me anyway. Forgive me when I become impatient in prayer. Remind me of this wonderful teaching that encourages me to keep on praying. Help me to claim the promise that you will hear and act—and to trust you with the timing. And when I find myself in a spiritual desert, remind me to share my feelings with trusted Christian friends and colleagues. Amen.

TEAM *Matters*

OBJECTIVE: to remind leaders to continue to pray, even when God seems silent, and to trust that God will bring about justice.

ITEMS NEEDED: two photocopies of the script on pages 39 and 40.

PREPARATION: Before this session, recruit two volunteers to play the roles of the judge and the widow. Ask them to bring simple props, such as a head scarf for the widow and a judge's robe, cell phone, and briefcase for the judge.

ACT IT OUT Using the script on pages 39 and 40, help this text come alive by acting it out with the two volunteers you recruited before the meeting.

READ & REFLECT After acting out the Scripture, ask everyone to read Luke 18:1-8. Then encourage participants to reflect upon this Scripture and the activity by forming groups of two or three and discussing the questions on pages 41 and 42. You may want them to discuss as many questions as time allows or select certain questions that you feel are especially relevant to your group. You may also give everyone a photocopy of the questions to facilitate discussion. ■

Enriching THE EXPERIENCE

Provide tools for participants to use to enhance their prayer lives. For example, you could provide personal devotional books (such as *Portals of Prayer* or Guideposts magazine), books on different types of prayer (such as *Prayers From the Heart* by Richard J. Foster), or something that has been developed especially for your congregation (such as a list of people in need of prayer or your congregation's prayer requests).

Script

Leader: Our story today is about a widow *(enter widow)* and a judge *(enter judge)*. This judge *(proudly walking around, perhaps with a briefcase and talking on a cell phone)* was a prominent figure in the community. He had a reputation for being strict and often inhumane, for he seemed to care little about human circumstances and only about carrying out the letter of the law. Now the widow *(hunched over, meekly cowering near the judge)* had approached the judge for help in resolving a dispute in which she had been treated unfairly. Much to her disappointment, the judge had disregarded her case, for without proper representation, he would not even hear her case. Seeking mercy and a second chance *(widow timidly approaches judge)*, the widow approached the judge.

Widow: *(Dropping to her knees)* Oh, most honorable judge, have mercy on me. Grant justice against my adversary.

Leader: But the judge showed her no mercy. Too busy to bother with her, he simply walked away. *(Judge contemptuously walks away.)* But the widow didn't stop. She sought the judge again.

Widow: *(Hands clasped together, prayerlike)* Oh, most honorable judge, have mercy on me. I am a widow, alone and with little to my name, but this one thing I desire. Please, I beg of you, grant me justice against my adversary.

Leader: This time the judge stopped long enough to hear the widow's plea, but he remained without compassion and, walking away, simply disregarded her request. *(Judge walks away.)* Finally, with her last ounce of strength, the widow approached the judge one more time.

→

Script

(continued)

Widow: Oh, most honorable judge, have mercy on me. I do not have the ability to present my case to you properly in court, but my motives are honest, and it is justice I seek. Please, I beg of you, grant me justice against my adversary.

Judge: Woman, you are old and without means. While your case is of no interest to me, your persistence has gotten my attention. I will grant you justice, as you have asked, simply because I want you to leave me alone. Consider it done, and be on your way.

Widow: *(Bowing, whispers)* Thank you.

(Widow and judge exit.)

Leader: And so the widow's wishes were granted. Now hear the Word of our Lord: "Listen to what the unjust judge says. And will not God bring about justice for his chosen ones, who cry out to him day and night? Will he keep putting them off? I tell you, he will see that they get justice, and quickly" (Luke 18:6-8a). So to all who desire justice, cry out to the Lord. For if an ungodly man can grant justice even when he does not care for humanity, imagine how much more our Father in heaven, who loves us, will be just and hear our prayers.

Getting REAL

1. In this story, God uses a man "who neither feared God nor cared about men" as an instrument of justice.

- Have you ever experienced a time God used such a person to answer one of your prayers? What happened?
- Why might God use such people?
- What was the judge's intention when he helped the widow?
- Do the intentions of the person helping have to be kind in order to serve God?
- Have you ever been in the role of the judge? How would you describe that experience?

Today, take some time to pray for people like the judge. Thank God for their role in our lives, but also pray for them to come to know God.

2. Have you ever found yourself in a position similar to the widow's, longing for someone's attention, to be heard, to find justice?

- How would you describe the experience? Why did you persist?
- Have you been as persistent with God? What drove you to approach God with your request time and time again?
- How did God meet your need?
- Was your prayer finally answered?
- Was it answered the way you wanted it to be?
- Were you exhausted or encouraged by the process?

Sometimes the journey of praying is as important, if not more important, than the ultimate answer. For the next month, write about your prayer time in a journal. Then review the journal entries, and try to discern what God might be teaching you.

→

Getting REAL

(continued)

3. How's your prayer life?

- Are you taking your concerns and joys to God, day and night?
- If someone asked you what he or she could do to help you with your prayer life, what would you say?
- What does your prayer life need—discipline, new styles of prayer, a Bible study on prayer, a community to pray with?

Once you have identified a need in your prayer life, find a resource that might help you. Commit to take one action step this week to enhance your personal discipline of prayer.

4. Are you a member of a safe community in which you can discuss your spiritual life?

- Do you pray within that community?
- Do the other members of the community join you on your prayer journey?
- What has been or could be the benefit of such a group in your life?
- Who are some people who might partner with you in such an adventure?

One gift we can give one another is to pray those persistent prayers together. In your group, share one prayer request you would like the others to join you in praying for the next ten days. Check in with one another at the end of that time. If you'd like to continue this practice, ask four or five people to form a prayer group with you.

Section Two
THE CALL

Between our experiences and growth in relationship with Jesus Christ and the expression of that through leadership comes the call. The call is the invitation and opportunity for leaders to exercise their gifts in a particular setting.

It has been my experience that the Holy Spirit often reactivates leaders by affirming our call. This can come in a renewed vision for ministry in our present situation, or it can be a call to move on. How can we reclaim our holy calling? How do we know when God is calling us to another part of the Lord's vineyard?

Such questions are invitations for dialogue with the Spirit of God and others within our communities. But those discussions are best framed within the context of Scripture. These devotions seek to both reassert the sacred nature of the call of a Christian leader and to place our reflections on our calling within the context of particular passages of the Bible. In so doing, I hope that Christian leaders will be better equipped not only to reflect upon their personal calling but also to talk to other leaders about theirs.

Something wondrous occurs when Christian leaders reclaim their call. The Spirit re-energizes us. Our service, no matter what its context, takes on new meaning and power. We are better able to focus our gifts and energies for the growth of Christ's Church.

So I invite you to reconsider your call—and to invite others into a sacred conversation about theirs.

7 KEY ELEMENTS OF THE CALL

Acts 13:1-5

I was just walking out of our office building. I was going to the worship center where I would address a few hundred Christian leaders for the first time. I had been at Prince of Peace for a short time, and I was nervous.

As I stepped out of the doorway, I stopped dead in my tracks. "Who are you to be doing this?" an inner voice accused. "After all, you are just a little boy from Richland, Washington. What could you possibly have to say to these women and men?"

As I stood there, reeling from the question, I heard my spirit say, "I have been called. God would not have called if I didn't have the gifts for this work. God will give me what I require." And I confidently crossed the parking lot.

Christian leaders are called by God. The call is, ultimately, the foundation for our leading and serving in Christ's church. When the devil wants to silence us or undo our ability to witness for the Savior, he will often attack our call. This can come internally, as it did that afternoon for me. Or it can come externally from those who challenge our leadership or our qualifications to lead. Our Lord seeks to equip us for such challenges with a clear understanding of the call itself. In Acts 13, the Holy Spirit gives us a remarkable picture of the three key elements of a biblical call.

The first element is an inner stirring. "In the church at Antioch there were prophets and teachers: Barnabas, Simeon called Niger, Lucius of Cyrene, Manaen (who had been brought up with Herod the tetrarch) and Saul. While they were worshipping the Lord and fasting, the Holy Spirit said, 'Set apart for me Barnabas and Saul for the work to which I have called them' " (Acts 13:1-2).

The fact that they were in prayer and fasting suggests that there was an inner stirring in the souls of these early church leaders. The Spirit of God was about to do something and began by stirring the hearts of these men to listen for and act on what God would tell them to do.

Frequently, the inner stirring begins in the heart of an individual. We become dissatisfied with what we are doing. We begin to long for something of more substance. There is an inner, spiritual turbulence that prepares us to receive the call. Saul and Barnabas were certainly stirred in that manner. Their response to this call was immediate: "So after they had fasted and prayed, they placed their hands on them and sent them off" (Acts 13:3). Saul and Barnabas went because the Spirit of God had been preparing them for the work to which they had just been called. The first key element of a call is an inner stirring.

The second key element is the affirmation of the community. I can't help but notice how the call is affirmed in the ritual actions of fasting, prayer, and then the laying on of hands. No matter how strong the inner stirring, if the community of faith does not affirm it, there is no call. The Bible is consistent and clear on this point.

THERE IS AN INNER, SPIRITUAL TURBULENCE THAT PREPARES US TO RECEIVE THE CALL.

When we leaders have had our inner stirrings confirmed by the community of faith, we can rest assured that the call hasn't been just a good idea or a misguided desire on our part. And later, when the devil challenges our call, God reminds us of this external affirmation to renew our confidence. Saul and Barnabas were *sent by the church*...their personal calls had been affirmed by the larger church.

This leads us to the third key element of the call to Christian leadership, an opportunity: "The two of them, sent on their way by the Holy Spirit, went down to Seleucia and sailed from there to Cyprus. When they arrived at Salamis, they proclaimed the word of God in the Jewish synagogues" (Acts 13:4-5a). There was an opportunity, which the Spirit led them to pursue. This opportunity confirmed their personal inner stirrings as well as the community's affirmation and commission. Without an opportunity, there is no actualized call. The opportunity is God's final confirmation of our call to leadership.

As Christian leaders, we know not only that some of our decisions will be challenged but also that the very call itself will be questioned. As we are secure in our understanding of God's call, we can withstand the tests of time and the changes that our call will naturally endure. Saul and Barnabas were not called to minister together indefinitely; there came a time when they parted company. Saul was not called to stay in Cyprus indefinitely; he was ultimately called to three great missionary journeys and would take the gospel to the ends of the Roman Empire. But the basis for his confidence in the call was his relationship with the risen Christ and the threefold call process outlined in Acts 13.

That was the source of my spiritual confidence that afternoon as I stood frozen on the sidewalk. God had stirred my heart to be open to his call. The community of faith gathered at Prince of Peace had affirmed the call, and God had made this opportunity available to me. Now I was simply required to obediently follow through on the call I had received.

With such spiritual confidence, I believe we can be open to growing in our calls. Someone once wrote, "God doesn't call the equipped. God equips the called." I understand that to mean that when the three key elements of call are present, we have the basic gifts required for the work at hand, but God will have more for us to learn as we serve. The opportunity is not just about the work. It is also about us: our spiritual growth, the development of our souls.

I have learned that if God is stretching me, I am in the right place. The teaching of the Holy Spirit continues as we live out our call. Otherwise, we can rust out, become bored, and slide into dissatisfaction. Christian confidence and boredom do not coexist within the heart of the called leader for long. Either our confidence wins out and we are called to stretch into new areas of ministry where we serve, or God uses our boredom to stir our hearts to be open to new opportunities. In either case, the call of God remains the firm foundation for our work until God calls us to eternity and we receive the promises in which we have lived and served.

LEADERSHIP PRAYER

Lord Jesus, send your Holy Spirit again today to confirm the call you have given me. Help me not to be surprised when your call is challenged by the evil one. Instead, plant me firmly in your faithfulness. Help me trust that, if my call in this place is over, you will provide another opportunity, as you did with Paul. And for as long as I serve you, help me be open to the continued tutoring of your Holy Spirit. In your name I pray, amen.

TEAM *Matters*

Objective: for leaders to understand the three elements of a calling and to discover their own personal calling.

Items needed: paper and a pencil for each participant.

EXPLAIN Use this activity to help participants deepen their understanding of their calling. The activity is a personal one. It's a chance for the members of your team to pause, quiet themselves, and listen to God.

READ & JOURNAL The reflection questions on pages 47-48 are separated into three sections. Encourage participants to read Acts 13:1-5 before working on each section and to use the questions as starting points for contemplation, prayer, and/or journaling. Gently guide the time, without rushing but moving the group from one section to another. End by laying hands on each person and praying for him or her.

Getting REAL

The disciplines of discipleship are intended not only for our personal journeys but also to prepare us for works of ministry. Out of our life of discipleship comes a calling by God. Today we are going to take some time to think about our calling.

1. What's stirring in your soul?

- What ministry issues keep getting your attention?
- Review events of the past month, and make a list of the pressing issues in your life. You might list *causes* such as unwed mothers, poverty, and education. Your list could be *ministry-oriented* and contain items such as studying God's Word, caring for the sick, or teaching children about Jesus. Your list might include a *target audience* such as elderly people who don't know Jesus or leaders in other countries who are attempting to establish new churches. Your desire might be to change the world or to quietly serve where you are. Regardless of the scale or focus of the items on your list, be open to the stirrings in your heart and what they might mean for your calling. Choose one or two items on your list, and explore them more deeply by applying these questions:
- What is the driving force behind the stirrings in your heart?
- What can you do to more clearly discern or define these stirrings?
- What resources are available to you that can make these stirrings a reality?
- How would these stirrings advance God's work in the world?
- What gifts do you have that would help you serve in that ministry?
- What experiences have prepared you to minister in that way?

2. What affirmation are you getting from others?

- Are any of these stirrings being identified by those around you?
- Are you part of a community that has similar passions or ministry desires?
- How might you connect with others with similar passions?
- Have you shared your ideas with others?
- How have they responded?
- Were they excited?
- What were their concerns?

➛

(continued)

- How were Barnabas' and Saul's calls affirmed by others? (See Acts 13:1-5.)
- What did Barnabas and Saul do to help them move their call forward?
- Think of three steps you can take to discover if others affirm your call.

3. Is there an opportunity to pursue this stirring?

- Do you see places where this stirring could become a reality? Is the need great enough to require God's help?
- Do you know of people who might join in this ministry?
- Have you talked with them about it?
- What was their response?
- Do you feel this leading is of God? Why?
- What obstacles stand in the way of moving forward?
- Do you think these obstacles are of God or of the devil?
- How might you discern the difference?
- Are you being obedient in heeding this call?
- How do you know?
- Name four things you can specifically pray for so that you may be confident that this stirring is a call from God.

Pray about those things for the next ten days.

8 RELATIONSHIP... NOT INSTITUTIONS

Matthew 28:16-20

I've been embarrassed about it for some time now. All of the excuses I have made for my misunderstanding and misapplication of this well-known Scripture just don't seem to hold water. The truth is that I just didn't see it. For years I read this text with this translation in my mind: "All authority in heaven and on earth has been given to me. Therefore go and make *members* of all nations" (Matthew 28:18b and 19a). I now know that this is not what the Savior said. I also know that for a significant portion of my ministry, I've responded to the Great Commission as if that were what Jesus commanded.

I believed that I fulfilled that command of Christ by making members of my church. I assumed that a person's membership in the congregation automatically confirmed his or her discipleship. Unfortunately, that isn't always the case. I have met wonderful people of God who were members of churches and for whom that membership was the natural extension of their discipleship. On the other hand, I have met members of my own church for whom membership seemed to mean a better deal when it came time for a child to be married or a family member to be buried. Any resemblance to discipleship was purely accidental.

Unfortunately, this led to two significant mistakes in my ministry. The first was that I put the institution of the church before the spiritual growth and vitality of the followers of Jesus Christ. Interesting. There is nothing in the Great Commission that speaks of institutional health. In fact, I have come to believe that by caring for the spiritual journey of the believer, the institutional health of the church is guaranteed. The church doesn't exist for itself. We gather in community to glorify God and contribute to the spiritual health and development of those who are called to follow Jesus. So, it's about relationship...not institutions.

The second mistake I made with this perspective of ministry is that I had low expectations of God's people. My denomination has for decades defined a member as someone who has attended worship or given *once in a given year.* What does that have to do with following Jesus Christ? If there is a cross in that expectation, it is at most a very minimal one!

THE CHURCH DOESN'T EXIST FOR ITSELF.

I have had the privilege of asking groups of Christian business people the following question: Do you believe that the church tolerates behaviors that business would never tolerate? The unanimous response has been *yes*.

The consequence of minimal expectations of Christians is that we have allowed a chasm to develop between what we believe and how we live. Raising expectations for disciples of Jesus is not perfectionism; it is the expectation that the gap between our beliefs and how we live will be narrowed and, by God's grace, bridged. That bridge can only be constructed with a clear understanding of God's grace. In other words, Jesus makes that bridge for us by his presence in every aspect of our lives. That is the promise in this disciple-making commission: "And surely I am with you always..." (Matthew 28:20b).

One inadvertent consequence of focusing on membership is that we begin to think that we meet God only or mostly in church. As a result, we can so easily miss the spiritual treasures that our Lord sows into every day of our lives.

Fernando is just such a treasure. I met him at the health club where we both work out. A hard-talking man who complained to me about the child support he had to pay his ex-wife, Fernando seemed to be a classic secular male. We became acquaintances and then friends. I began to look for him at the club and, apparently, he for me. Then one day he asked what I do for a living, and when he found out that I am a pastor, his conversation changed.

I didn't see him again for about six weeks. I began to pray that God would connect us again so that I could invite him to church. Then, by *coincidence*, we met late in the day at the club. After we had greeted each other, but before I could say anything else, Fernando asked if he could come to my church. He shared a bit of his life story and said that God was calling him back to a deep faith.

I don't know if Fernando will find a church home with us or not. But it isn't really about that. My prayer is that he will find a community of faith within which his personal walk with Jesus Christ can grow.

Through this story and so many others, I've learned that *coincidences* are actually *God incidents*. The call of Christian leaders is to make disciples, not members. When I understood that, I began to understand the remarkable truth that there is not a separation of sacred and secular. In fact, by faith the *secular* is transformed into that *sacred* space in which we meet the acting, loving God of Jesus Christ.

THE CALL OF CHRISTIAN LEADERS IS TO MAKE DISCIPLES, NOT MEMBERS.

One of the great gifts of deinstitutionalizing the Great Commission is that we discover the freedom of a *kingdom mentality*. It's not about *my* congregation any longer. We are not in competition with other Christian leaders. The goal is to increase the number of disciples in Christ's church, in whatever particular context that may take.

I confess to one of the great sins of the church: pastoral jealousy. I have looked at the growth and success of other pastors and felt pangs of jealousy and judgment. I have come to believe that such sin is a natural outcome of a membership-based ministry.

The call of the Savior is to bear one another's burdens and celebrate one another's successes. I believe we Christian leaders are called to a kingdom mentality that can free us from pastoral and ministerial jealousies or at least help us more honestly confront them and repent of them. Then we are released from the burden of trying to make everyone happy within our ministries—a task we soon discover is impossible.

Ultimately, the Great Commission is about a relationship with Jesus Christ. That relationship will call us into community and, as we tend that relationship within our congregations, our institutions will grow stronger and more vibrant. And that will give great glory to God.

LEADERSHIP PRAYER

Lord Jesus, forgive me for the jealousy I have felt when others have succeeded in ministry. Remind me that I labor in your vineyard. This isn't about *my* church; it's about *your* church. Help me see with kingdom eyes and trust that you will provide for the institutional church that serves that kingdom. Amen.

TEAM *Matters*

OBJECTIVE: to remind leaders that God calls them to foster spiritual growth in others, not to make members of congregations; to discover the freedom that comes with a kingdom mentality.

ITEMS NEEDED: for each participant, a photocopy of the questions on pages 52-53, paper (or a journal), a pencil, and a blank card to be used for a prayer request.

REFLECT & SHARE Tell participants that you will read Matthew 28:16-20 aloud twice. The first time, ask them to listen for the role leaders are to play in discipling others. After a time of reflection, ask participants to share their insights with the group. The second time you read Matthew 28:16-20, have people listen for the sins that block them from discipling others.

JOURNAL Use the questions on pages 52-53 to prompt participants to journal about this aspect of the text. (Distribute photocopies of the questions as well as blank cards for them to use for prayer requests as they delve into the questions.)

IMAGINE Ask participants to imagine what the world would be like if everyone worked together to build up God's kingdom. Close in prayer. ■

Getting REAL

This week, practice focusing your time on helping people grow spiritually, and note how that focus changes your perspective on ministry. Begin by noting on a blank card the name of a person and your prayer request for him or her. Before you leave, exchange cards with someone.

Now write your responses to the following questions:

1. What's your priority: your church or the people?

- How does your time reflect that commitment?
- How do you balance organizational issues and the needs of individuals?
- What's the role of a leader in a kingdom-based ministry?
- As you listened to Matthew 28:16-20, what words jumped out at you?
- What were the disciples doing during this time?
- What promises did Jesus give them?
- Can you be a leader in such a ministry?
- What are your fears about such a ministry? What excites you about it?

2. What are the sins that block you from living the Great Commission?

- Are they pride or jealousy?
- Are they fear or lack of faith?
- Has being a leader in this ministry inflated your ego?
- Has it given you power or influence?
- How have you used your leadership role?
- Has being a leader become a stumbling block in your relationship with Christ? How?
- What are the sins that block this ministry from living the Great Commission?
- How deeply ingrained are these sins?
- What would it take to remove them?
- Does this challenge push you out of your comfort zone?
- How does that make you feel?

➛

(continued)

This week consider the sins that block you from living the Great Commission, and present them to God in prayer each day. Be willing to allow God to change this aspect of your life.

3. How would this ministry be different if everyone in it adopted a kingdom mentality?

- What would leaders focus their efforts on?
- What would the rewards be?
- What would the downside be?
- If you focused on discipling people, who would you focus on first? Why?
- How would your energy be spent?

Imagine this new world in detail. Come up with a word or phrase that captures this picture for you. Write it on a piece of paper, and hang it from your car's rearview mirror or in your office. Every time you see it, let it be a reminder to work toward this new world.

9 EYES ON THE GOAL
Luke 9:51-62

"I want to finish well," my pastoral colleague and friend said.

Several pastors and I were reflecting on yet another pastor who had fallen. What a great ministry he had led in a large metropolitan area in the Northeast! We listened as my friend shared the phone call he had received, the request for prayers, and the repentant sorrow that accompanied the affair's publicity. This man's ministry was lost; his family was in utter disarray. His marriage was probably over. And the sorrow that lay on our hearts was heavy indeed.

It isn't that we weren't sympathetic to our fallen colleague. We were. There wasn't a person at that table of pastors who couldn't relate a story of temptation during a time of vulnerability. So we prayed for our colleague—and for one another. And we encouraged one another to keep our eyes on the goal of finishing strong.

In each of the Gospels, a dramatic moment is described in which it is clear that Jesus knew he was going to the cross. No other Gospel writer records this as dramatically as Luke. We read twice in three verses Luke's identification of this turning point in the earthly life of Jesus: "As the time approached for him to be taken up to heaven, *Jesus resolutely set out for Jerusalem*. And he sent messengers on ahead, who went into a Samaritan village to get things ready for him; but the people there did not welcome him, *because he was heading for Jerusalem*" (Luke 9:51-53). The language of the italicized text is translated in the New Revised Standard Version as "set his face to go to Jerusalem" and again "his face was set toward Jerusalem."

SIN IS A SHORT-TERM SOLUTION TO A LONG-TERM PROBLEM.

Jesus turned his complete attention toward his goal. He knew that from this moment on, no matter what happened, where he went, or whom he met along the way, his eyes were on the cross.

With this in mind, the rest of this remarkable text makes a great deal of sense. The rejection of the Samaritan village was a minor distraction to Jesus. No wonder he brushed off the anger of two of his closest friends, James and John. Their anger didn't merit Jesus' attention in light of his clear focus on Jerusalem.

The teachings in Luke 9:57-62 become crystal clear in light of this focus. Verse 62 summarizes the point of the text. Jesus said, "No one who puts his hand to the plow and looks back is fit for service in the kingdom of God." Nothing, not even the burial of loved ones, ought to get in the way of the final goal of the kingdom of God. Jesus spoke of himself. He also spoke to us.

As my colleagues and I talked that afternoon, this lesson came to mind. Through the tragic lens of our colleague's sin, we began to focus on eternity. Christian leaders know that sin is a short-term solution to a long-term problem. We desire to feel good, to solve an immediate difficulty without considering the future. Like a sailor lost at sea, we see only the next wave, not the land just on the horizon. So we act in the immediate without reference to the eternal. But Christian leaders know our Lord calls us to service not just for today, or even just for tomorrow. We are called to a lifetime of service.

Jesus refused to be distracted by the immediate at the cost of the ultimate. Whether his present was defined by rejection by an entire village in Samaria or the praise of would-be followers, his focus was on his calling. And the Savior understood that this call had a heavenly time frame.

Leaders can learn from this text that even seemingly appropriate responses may be set aside when the call is at stake. On the surface James and John's response seems to be righteous indignation. After all, the Samaritans were rejecting the Messiah! But the call was more important than that. The requests to bury a father and simply say farewell to loved ones both seem appropriate, even sensible, requests. But they were rejected because they compromised commitment to the call.

Remembering Jesus' single-minded focus on the call helps me quickly put rejection as well as praise in its proper place. When people leave Prince of Peace for another ministry, the rejection I feel is real. But asking what is at stake helps me work through it. If what is at stake is their own spiritual health and well-being, then it's not about me, and my call is not compromised by the self-punishment of excessive guilt. On the other hand, if I am praised for a ministry activity, I again ask, "What is at stake?" If accepting the praise compromises my understanding that my call is from Christ and through him I can accomplish much, then I remember that the praise is the temporary and that it is the eternal I must focus on.

IT'S NOT ABOUT ME.

I wonder what the disciples thought of Jesus' single-minded commitment. I wonder how the crowds that seemed to always gather around him, even in the most remote areas, interpreted his intensity of purpose. And I wonder how those around us would react to such an unwavering sense of purpose.

I suspect that some admired Jesus' goal orientation. I also imagine that some turned from the Savior because he wasn't as responsive or sensitive as they would have liked. Perhaps even disciples like James and John felt put off by him. Only in the light of the Resurrection did his behavior make sense.

So also will Christian leaders be misunderstood. But how we serve, how we live our own discipleship and follow the call as we understand it, can only be fully known in light of the end of our story.

Keeping our eyes on the goal is our faithful attempt to put today in the context of forever. I know we can't always do that well—that's why we have a forgiving Lord. But it certainly helps us resist temptation, even as we ache for those who cannot. Is there any goal worthy of our call other than to finish well? I don't think so.

LEADERSHIP PRAYER

Lord Jesus, you resolutely turned to Jerusalem and kept your eye on the goal of finishing your ministry well. Today I ask that your Spirit would create the same kind of focus within me. Let me put this day, with all of its potential for praise or rejection, within the context of your call. Help me to resist the evil one, shrug off distractions, and finish well. In your holy name, amen.

TEAM *Matters*

Objective: for leaders to understand the importance of having an eternal goal and of keeping their eyes fixed upon it.

Items needed: a quiet room with lighting that may be dimmed, a CD of soft music or relaxing nature sounds, a CD player, a photocopy of the questions on page 58 for each participant, paper (or a journal for each person), and pencils.

CHALLENGE Ask participants to get comfortable and close their eyes as you take them on an imaginary journey. Read the following scenario aloud:

IMAGINE "Leave the concerns of the world at the door, and free yourself to travel to a new place. This place is actually a time: the final few days of your life. You have been given a gift. The gift is to spend the final days of your life wherever and with whomever you choose, doing whatever you like. You are not ill or suffering in any way. You have simply been given the gift of time with those who are most important to you, doing what you most value. Note where you are. Are you in your home? somewhere outdoors? a favorite vacation spot? a place you've been before or a place you've always wanted to visit? Who is with you? There is no limit to the guest list; anyone might be at this gathering. What family members do you see? How do you greet them when you first see their faces? What voices from your past are there? What memories do they stir within you? Do they remind you of good days or bad? Do you

TEAM *Matters*

(continued)

harbor ill will toward anyone there? What would you say to those people? Notice that the tone is upbeat. What are people talking about? What are people doing? Who's interacting with whom? What are you doing? What is your mood?

"The gathering shifts. People begin to move toward a large dining hall where a huge banquet has been prepared. You, of course, are seated at the head of the room with your closest friends and family around you. Name those people. Your host greets everyone, and then people begin to enjoy the wonderful food set before them. Spontaneously, people stand up to share words or thoughts about you—your accomplishments, your passions, your joyful times, your sorrow-filled times, humorous moments, significant family moments, the impact you've had on the lives of others. For some reason, this doesn't embarrass you; in fact, you rather enjoy this review of your life. At times you join in the laughter. Other times, tears roll down your face. Between stories, you sit back and soak in the variety of experiences that have made up your life.

"The meal ends, and people begin to call it a night and make their way to their rooms. You mingle with them, thanking them for being there and for their thoughtful words. Soon you are alone in the room. Now you are faced with a decision. Ahead of you is one week, your final seven days on earth. What will you do? Who will you spend time with?"

JOURNAL Allow participants several moments to imagine this scenario. Then ask them to describe in writing how they felt during the "journey" and what they would do with their final days. Use the questions on page 58 to guide them.

READ & APPLY Finally, read Luke 9:51-62 aloud, and ask participants to compare their imagined final days with those of Jesus. Ask them to consider Jesus' focus and priorities during his last week. What can they learn from this comparison? ■

Getting REAL

1. Describe the people at your gathering.

- Identify them; then describe what they were doing and how you felt about their presence.
- Highlight some of the stories that were shared, including humorous as well as somber ones.
- Was anyone there with whom you had unfinished business?
- What would compel you to deal with those issues?

2. Did certain themes surface for you?

- Did the people who were there or the stories they shared reflect your values?
- What impact did the surroundings have on you?
- Do those surroundings say something about what's important to you?
- Make a list of your core values.
- Think about ways your life reflects those values and things you'd like to change so your actions will more clearly reflect them.

3. Did the fact that this gathering was a part of your final days affect you? How?

- Did this fact change your attitude?
- Did it cause your focus to be different?
- Did it feel like a gift or a burden?
- In Jesus' final days, his words and actions became more pointed. Are your actions clearly focused on a certain goal?
- Did knowing that your time was limited create a sense of urgency?
- If you lived with that kind of urgency now, how would your life change?

10 CONFIDENT INTERCESSION
Luke 7:1-10

My family and I were in the last stages of preparing for a long trip when a pastor friend stopped by on the spur of the moment. We delayed our departure and spent some time with him. When it was time to leave, we invited him into our circle of prayer. We prayed for safe travel for him and ourselves. We prayed for his family, and we prayed that God would bless him in his ministry. After we said amen, he asked, "Do you always pray that way?"

"What do you mean?" I asked.

"Well, I never pray specifically for safety for me or my family when we travel. Nor do I pray for any specific blessing. I just put it all in God's hands. Any other way seems selfish."

"Well, do you want a safe journey and specific blessings?" I asked.

"Oh, yes," he replied.

"Then who are you fooling? Do you think God knows what you really desire or not? And if God knows, isn't it more honest to ask for it and then to trust God with whatever comes?"

Luke 7:1-10 includes two remarkable affirmations. Both are in response to bold requests for our Lord to act. The first affirmation came to those who interceded for the centurion: "The centurion heard of Jesus and sent some elders of the Jews to him, asking him to come and heal his servant. When they came to Jesus, they pleaded earnestly with him, 'This man deserves to have you do this, because he loves our nation and has built our synagogue.' So Jesus went with them" (verses 3-6a).

There is no record that Jesus debated the merits of the request. Rather, in response to the Jewish leaders' bold request on behalf of the centurion, "Jesus went with them."

> OUR CONFIDENCE IS BASED ON THE HEART OF JESUS CHRIST.

One call of leadership is to boldly come before God on behalf of others. This boldness is not dependent upon our worthiness or even theirs. Rather, our confidence is based on the heart of Jesus Christ. I wonder how much energy those early Jewish leaders expended trying to convince Jesus to heal the centurion's servant when our Lord needed only to be asked. And I wonder how often we restrain our prayers because we are afraid to ask.

I understand this tendency. I have often prayed for healing for people whose diseases were deemed incurable. These prayers for healing were based on the power of God to do anything God chooses to do. But, given the prognoses, I have had to then place these people in the care of the eternal Creator, who offers us our final healing in death itself. I hope I wasn't fudging! I just wanted to be bold and honest before God—asking for what we really wanted. At the same time, we learn that we rarely understand when or why God will do a miracle…and why he won't.

The second affirmation in this passage was for the centurion. When he learned that Jesus was coming, he made his confidence in Jesus abundantly clear: "He [Jesus] was not far from the house when the centurion sent friends to say to him: 'Lord, don't trouble yourself, for I do not deserve to have you come under my roof. That is why I did not even consider myself worthy to come to you. But say the word, and my servant will be healed. For I myself am a man under authority, with soldiers under me. I tell this one, "Go," and he goes; and that one, "Come," and he comes. I say to my servant, "Do this," and he does it' " (Luke 7:6b-8).

The centurion boldly asked for and then claimed Jesus' healing! Our Lord responded with one of his greatest recorded affirmations: "I tell you, I have not found such great faith even in Israel" (Luke 7:9b).

I doubt that the centurion's request was purely selfless. This was a servant for whom he prayed. Yes, the text tells us he valued him highly. But he was, nonetheless, a servant—someone who would serve the centurion if he were healed.

> IF WE BASE OUR CONFIDENCE UPON THE SELF-LESS PURITY OF OUR PRAYERS, FEW PRAYERS WOULD EVER BE UTTERED.

The nature of prayer may often seem murky to Christian leaders. If we base our confidence upon the selfless purity of our prayers, few prayers would ever be uttered. We pray for ourselves (which the centurion did in a roundabout way) with boldness because our God loves us just as we are. This boldness lays the foundation for our trust in God's ultimate response, whatever it might be. We are called to pray for ourselves with as much confidence as we pray for others. The author of the book of Hebrews puts it this way: "Let us then approach the throne of grace with confidence, so that we may receive mercy and find grace to help us in our time of need" (Hebrews 4:16).

I have often wondered if Jesus' affirmation of the centurion wasn't also an instruction for Jesus' followers. It's as if our Lord was saying, "See? That's the way you do it. Just let me know what you need, and then trust me for it." As long as the focus of our trust is Jesus Christ, then whatever selfishness is in the prayer will ultimately serve our faith and give glory to God.

Perhaps the overarching lesson for us is that we are called to be in a *real relationship* with God in Jesus Christ. Let us exercise as little pretense or attempted perfection as possible. Let's just say it simply and then trust. That's what the Jewish leaders did in this text. That's what the centurion did. And who wouldn't love to hear the Savior speak that wondrous affirmation about us: "I tell you, I have not found such great faith even in Israel"?

LEADERSHIP PRAYER

Lord Jesus, I want to be honest when I pray. I sometimes feel that if I am honest, my prayers will be selfish and unhealthy. Forgive me. Thank you for inviting me to be real with you. Help me to trust that, in your eternal wisdom and love, you will sort out all my prayers and do what is best. Thank you for the affirmations in this passage of Scripture. Help me to claim them in my own life. Amen.

TEAM *Matters*

Objective: for leaders to understand the significance of praying for others as well as bringing their own needs to God.

Items needed: paper (or a journal), a pencil, and a photocopy of the questions on page 62 for each participant.

CHALLENGE Read Luke 7:1-10 aloud. Explain that this devotion is intended to help participants explore the role of intercessory prayer in a Christian's life. Ask participants to make a list of people they would risk themselves to protect. After each name, have them describe a situation in which they may have interceded in that person's life. For example, someone may have questioned a doctor's diagnosis of a child's illness. Or perhaps someone spoke up for a colleague. Ask participants to identify what motivated them to step up to help these people. Ask them to write their motivations next to each incident. When everyone has finished, ask participants to review their lists and identify any themes that emerge.

APPLY & DISCUSS Ask participants to make a second list, this time of their own needs. After each need, have them write the names of people who have interceded on their behalf. Encourage participants to reflect upon this activity and the Scripture by forming groups of two or three and discussing the questions on page 62.

PRAY Ask everyone to share a prayer request with the group, and then ask for a volunteer to pray for that need right then. Continue this process until everyone who chooses to share has had the opportunity to do so. ■

1. Share with another person an experience in which you acted as an intercessor.

- What was the situation?
- What was the outcome?
- How were you affected by the process?
- Was the person aware of your intercessory role?
- What impact did your intercession have on your relationship with that person?

2. Jesus said to the centurion, "I have not found such great faith even in Israel." What place does faith have in our role as intercessors?

- How can we, as sinners, have the confidence to come before God, the creator of the universe, and ask for help?
- Have you ever refrained from asking God for something because you thought your request was trivial?
- How would you respond to the same situation now?
- How will this story affect your prayer life?
- How would you rate intercession as an aspect of leadership on a scale of one to ten, with one being not important and ten being very important? Why?

3. If you were to teach a lesson on this Bible story, what would be your main point?

- Who would be your target audience?
- How would you make the main point come alive for the audience?
- Can you think of stories from your own life that would illustrate this point? What are they?

Share this Bible story and your personal experiences with someone this week, and watch how he or she responds.

11 THE FREEDOM OF FORGIVENESS

Luke 17:1-10

I remember how queasy I felt when I saw her. She had publicly said things about me that were both unkind and untrue. Now I saw her in the sanctuary before worship. Anger welled up within me like bile in the back of the throat. The last thing I wanted to do was to greet her. But that was exactly what the Spirit was whispering in my heart to do. So, with a sigh, I approached her and said, "Hi, Joan." I tried to smile; I'm still not certain I succeeded.

Jesus commands us to forgive. In Luke 17:1-10, he makes it clear that his command has no real limits: "If your brother sins, rebuke him, and if he repents, forgive him. If he sins against you seven times in a day, and seven times comes back to you and says, 'I repent,' forgive him" (verses 3b-4). Seven is a symbolic number. In the Bible, *seven* always means *complete* or *whole.* So the gist of our Lord's teaching is that we are to forgive as many times as necessary until the relationship is whole.

WE ARE TO FORGIVE AS MANY TIMES AS NECESSARY UNTIL THE RELATIONSHIP IS WHOLE.

As Christian leaders, we assume that Jesus doesn't ask us to do anything that we cannot do. Nor will our Savior ask us to do that which is unhealthy for us or others. So this text prompts me to ask, "How can I do this?"

The disciples seem to have had a similar response. Their reaction to this teaching was not to challenge it but to express their sincere doubts about their abilities to obey it. They exclaimed, "Increase our faith!" (Luke 17:5b).

Indeed. A willingness to obey such a command would seem to require a great deal of faith. The apostles express our own concern: Is it really responsible to forgive so often and so willingly? Won't we become doormats? And what about the other person? Won't we be encouraging misbehavior?

The only answer Jesus gives in our text is a story about obedience, even when we are fatigued. So we pray for the ability to trust that Jesus will do what is good in us and through us when we forgive—again and again and again.

So we know that forgiveness is commanded by Christ. We are called to forgive and dare to trust that the Lord will make the forgiving life-giving. That's why increased faith is the right prayer. It means that I give my need to punish to the

Savior who judges all. I do this because my choosing to forgive is the point of my own judgment. Forgiveness for the Christian is not an option; it is a requirement.

When I walked away from Joan that day, my spirit was light. The anger was still there, but its power was diminished. And I understood that Jesus' command is an invitation to freedom: the freedom to unload an inner burden.

FORGIVENESS FOR THE CHRISTIAN IS NOT AN OPTION; IT IS A REQUIREMENT.

Do you remember the nine miners who were trapped for seventy-seven hours in a water-filled tunnel in the summer of 2002? They survived through a combination of teamwork, discipline, and sheer heart. When one became dangerously cold, the others surrounded him and shared their bodies' diminishing warmth. Then when another was chilled, they would turn and gather around him in warmth and support. This discipline brought them all through their dark ordeal. It's what they knew. They obeyed the rules of survival and were finally lifted in a wire basket into the freedom and light of day.

When we forgive, I think we are like those trapped miners. We gather around others to give them the warmth of God's love—a love we have already received. In the life-threatening chill of sin, the only warmth available is Christ's love and forgiveness. And we know that, if we don't forgive, we will succumb to that same chill. For when we sin, as we surely will, we will need the saints to gather around us in forgiveness—just as those miners received life-giving warmth from one another in a dark, waterlogged shaft.

I know that by approaching Joan I may have appeared foolish to those who knew what she had said and done. To those who didn't know of the inner command I had distinctly heard, approaching her may have seemed irresponsible or inauthentic.

Just like those miners. Can you imagine how they looked? Grown men in soiled, wet coveralls hugging in the dark. What they knew is what Jesus wants us to know about forgiveness: It is necessary for life.

The call is to obedience. The prayer for increased faith stems from a heartfelt desire to obey—to obey when we don't want to, don't understand the need for it, and don't want to relinquish our desire for the outcomes we think are appropriate.

As Christian leaders, we also understand this teaching within the context of the life and ministry of Jesus. It is clear that forgiveness in his life didn't mean a naive pretense in the face of sin. As Jesus passed through the crowd that was going to stone him, he didn't forgive them and then remain among them. He forgave and walked away. Sometimes we, too, are called to forgive and walk away from abusive, repetitive sin. But we still forgive. We shake off the dust…and walk away.

I have not spoken to Joan since that encounter before worship. I don't feel any need to do so. Apparently, she feels no need to speak to me, and if we did speak, I would choose my words carefully. Forgiveness isn't blind. It simply enables us to let go of an inner burden and welcomes us into the cool, fresh air of spiritual freedom.

FORGIVENESS ISN'T BLIND.

LEADERSHIP PRAYER

Lord Jesus, when I am unwilling to forgive, remind me of those trapped miners. Send your Spirit to tell me, once again, that forgiveness rescues me from the chill and darkness of sin. Hold before me the promise of the freedom forgiveness brings. Increase my faith. Help me practice the discipline of forgiveness. Amen.

TEAM *Matters*

Objective: to remind leaders that forgiveness is necessary for wholeness and that forgiveness is ultimately about letting the warmth of God's love into our lives.

Items needed: a source of water, "Gather at the River" (a song on Point of Grace's CD *Rarities & Remixes*), a CD player, and—for each participant—paper (or a journal), pencils, and a photocopy of the questions on page 66.

GATHER Gather for this activity at a baptismal font or another source of water such as a pond, river, or fountain.

READ Read Luke 17:3b-4 aloud. Remind participants of the importance of baptism in their faith journey by discussing the cleansing, life-giving characteristics of water.

REFLECT & PRAY Ask participants to come to the water, one by one, as you dip your hand in it and make a cross on each person's forehead, saying, "You are a child of God, marked with the cross of Christ forever." After anointing everyone in this way, invite participants to find a spot where they can be by themselves as they listen to "Gather at the River." Distribute the questions on page 66, and encourage participants to use these questions to spark private meditation. End with prayer. ■

1. Who do you need to forgive?

- What has been the cost of not forgiving this person?
- How has this situation affected your relationship?
- God commands us to forgive our brothers and sisters. What is preventing you from obeying this command?
- Do you see others as God's children? What does God want of his children?
- How do your relationships model Christian behavior?

2. What do you need to forgive yourself for?

- What sin is blocking you from God's lifeline of unconditional love?
- Do you need the renewal of God's life-giving water?
- Can you receive the gift of mercy Jesus gives you and accept God's love?
- Can you move beyond this situation and make a fresh start?

Pray for the strength to leave your sins at Jesus' feet.

3. "We gather around others to give them the warmth of God's love—a love we have already received. In the life-threatening chill of sin, the only warmth available is Christ's love and forgiveness." What is your response to this view of forgiveness?

- Do you feel the chill of sin in your life? How could forgiveness bring warmth to those situations?
- What can you do to make God's love evident in those situations?

Pray for God to show you how you might be an instrument of reconciliation.

12 IN PURSUIT OF ETERNITY

1 Timothy 6:6-13

"Why do most ministries fail?" he asked.

We had been talking, this mission planter from a different denomination and I, for nearly forty-five minutes. Now he was winding the interview down and had introduced the question with these words: "I know we have to end, but I'd like to ask what is, perhaps, my most important question. As I plant this church, I don't want to fail." Then he asked the question.

I thought for a few minutes and then responded, "I think there are probably two primary reasons. The first is lack of focus—Christian leaders who try to do everything for everyone. They don't know the specific purpose God has called them to accomplish through their ministry. The second reason follows on the first—lack of courage in leadership. Ministries often fail because the leader or leaders lack the courage to say no to the distractions and temptations that blur their focus."

In Paul's first letter to Timothy, he said, in effect, "Stay on track. Have the courage to be persistent in your pursuit of eternity." The text's actual words are "Fight the good fight of the faith. Take hold of the eternal life to which you were called when you made your good confession in the presence of many witnesses" (1 Timothy 6:12). This is the bull's-eye of Paul's remarkable charge to Timothy. The language here is wonderfully clear: The ultimate call for Timothy (and for us as Christian leaders) was to eternal life. Everything else will fade away. Only this final gift from the risen Savior will last forever.

THIS FOCUS ON THE POVERTY OF THE HUMAN CONDITION AND THE WEALTH OF GOD'S GRACE PUTS MONEY IN ITS PROPER PERSPECTIVE.

With this as the heart of this passage of Scripture, we can go both backward and forward for greater understanding of the spiritual truths within it. For example, we now can better understand Paul's words in 1 Timothy 6:6: "But godliness with contentment is great gain. For we brought nothing into the world, and we can take nothing out of it." Godliness (a holy character and life) is complete in contentment (peace in every circumstance). We can be content because we know we entered the world as paupers and will leave in the same manner. So Paul teaches that if we keep our eyes on the call to eternal life, then the poverty of both birth and death are illuminated by the great joy of God's gift to us.

This focus on the poverty of the human condition and the wealth of God's grace puts money in its proper perspective. Many people remember the words of 1 Timothy 6:10 as "Money is the root of all evil." The actual language is quite different. Paul actually wrote, "For the love of money is a root of all kinds of evil." From this it is clear that money, in and of itself, isn't the issue; it is the value we place on it.

It's all about focus. Ministries fail for the same reasons that lives fail: Our inner eyes wander from the object of true worth, and we give ourselves to things that fade, that lose their value over time. The material crowds out the spiritual. The joy of ministry gives way to the mundane. The passion for Jesus slips into an institutional focus on the budget. Or we simply spend our time in chaplaincy, performing religious functions to those in the church and failing to reach out to our communities in Jesus' name. Focus fades. Perspective slides. Vision dims.

I know how easy it is to become distracted and to lose focus. Once, my world shifted as a result of one phone call in which I was invited to consider another ministry opportunity. I agreed to pray about it. I went home and talked to my wife about it. Over the next few weeks, no matter how hard I tried to focus on the work at church, I was in turmoil. When I least expected it, the phone would ring and someone would ask me about it or people would bring it up in casual conversation. My world was interrupted by one distraction after another. I asked trusted colleagues at Prince of Peace to tell me if they thought my ministry was beginning to suffer.

WHATEVER THE CONTEXT, THE ULTIMATE CALL IS TO ETERNITY.

I didn't know how to move ahead. I wasn't sure which target I should pay attention to—let alone where the bull's-eye was! And in prayer I simply asked God to let me hear God's voice. The peace that finally came, after weeks of inner turmoil and prayer, was the result of focusing on the call. I remembered Paul's exhortation to Timothy: Whatever the context, the ultimate call is to eternity. The context in which we serve Christ may change; serving the Master with a confident claim on heaven will not.

And this has taught me a great leadership lesson. The various forms of our ministries can and will change. Even the vision toward which we strive for a particular ministry will shift. But the call to present to others the eternal gift of the gospel will never change.

So I have begun to ask myself how I'm doing at presenting eternity to others. I have begun to hold my activities and acquisitions up against the poverty of my condition and the richness of God's invitation in Christ Jesus. It makes a difference. The perspective of eternity is very different from the perspective of today, of this activity or that program. And I have found a remarkable freedom to learn and grow.

A friend recently lost his house in a matter of minutes. Lightning struck, and the dream home that he and his wife had recently built lit up like a torch. They were able to save a few meager possessions. He told me that, standing on the curb, looking at the burnt hulk that had been their home, they discovered an amazing freedom. With little or nothing left of their earthly goods, they stood with their children and grandchildren and realized how rich they still were. They had the Lord. They had their family. Everything else was expendable. He said that in retrospect it was one of the best things to ever happen to his family. They learned that so much of life can be stripped away from us in the blink of an eye. But God's eternal gifts remain.

SO MUCH OF LIFE CAN BE STRIPPED AWAY FROM US IN THE BLINK OF AN EYE. BUT GOD'S ETERNAL GIFTS REMAIN.

In his great hymn "A Mighty Fortress Is Our God," Martin Luther says it in these words: "Let goods and kindred go, this mortal life also; The body they may kill: God's truth abideth still."

It's a matter of focus, isn't it?

LEADERSHIP PRAYER

Lord Jesus, what a great calling you have given me! It is the very invitation to spend eternity with you. Thank you. When I am distracted by this world and all of its things, lift my vision to you; lift my vision to heaven. I thank you that I am yours and that, though everything else may change, this one fact will not. Amen.

TEAM *Matters*

Objective: for leaders to recognize what's temporary and what's eternal in their lives.

Items needed: index cards, a pen, and—for each participant—paper (or a journal), a pencil, and a photocopy of the questions on page 71.

Preparation: Before this session, create a set of twenty index cards for each participant. Write the following words on the cards, one word or phrase per card: *money, fame, love, joy, influence, savings account, family, cars, achievement, peace, promotions, awards, pleasure, authority, hugs, compassion, faith, ambition, grace,* and *life.*

CHALLENGE Give each participant a set of cards, and tell everyone to create two piles. In one pile, participants should place the cards that represent temporal values; in the other, eternal values. Ask them to do this individually. Then, when they've finished, ask them to pair up and compare their answers. Ask them to talk about the process they used in sorting and to explain their decisions.

DISCUSS Read 1 Timothy 6:6-13 aloud. Ask participants to reflect upon this Scripture and the activity by forming groups of two or three and discussing the questions on page 71. You may want them to discuss as many questions as time allows or select certain questions that you feel are especially relevant to your group. End the session by adapting the prayer on page 69 to your setting. ■

Enriching THE EXPERIENCE

Help participants use all the lessons in this section to more clearly define their own calling. Before the session, ask them to bring their notes or journal entries from the past five sessions. Then lead them through the following questions.

First Timothy 6:12b says to "take hold of the eternal life."

- **What do these words tell you about the focus of this life?**
- **How does this focus affect your call from God?**
- **Is this a short-term or long-term focus?**
- **Review your notes or journal entries from the past five sessions. Has your understanding of your call changed as a result of these lessons?**
- **How would you now describe your call as a disciple of Christ?**

Getting REAL

1. What things trap you? Money? Recognition? Talent? Power? Reread 1 Timothy 6:7-10, replacing the word *money* with the sin you've identified.

- How has this sin become a trap for you?
- What are some foolish and harmful desires that have come with this sin?
- Describe times it has caused you to wander from faith.
- Now reread 1 Timothy 6:11-12. What would happen if you replaced these traps with righteousness, godliness, faith, love, endurance, or gentleness?
- How would your life be different?
- What would happen to those foolish and harmful desires?
- Why does Paul mention "in the presence of many witnesses" in 1 Timothy 6:12? Why is that significant?

This week, be aware of the sins that trap you or lead you to harmful desires. Work to replace those sins with the attributes listed in 1 Timothy 6:11. Ask someone to keep you accountable for this and share your experience with that person at the end of seven days.

2. Compare 1 Timothy 6:7 ("For we brought nothing into the world, and we can take nothing out of it") with the popular bumper sticker "The one with the most toys wins." Both represent philosophies of life.

- Which end of the continuum are you nearer?
- Have you ever been completely without material goods? What was that like?
- What lessons can be learned from such times?
- Have you ever lived with plenty of material goods? What was that like?
- What lessons can be learned from those times?

Material goods and wealth are not evil, in and of themselves. Yet too often we become so wrapped up in these things that we miss opportunities to live the message of the gospel. Write a poem or a song that describes for you what it means to live with a focus on the eternal.

Section Three
VISION

Vision is focused passion. As Christian leaders exercise their gifts through their call, God inspires vision. This vision is born out of a leader's heartfelt desire to achieve great things for the kingdom of God. This longing to see Christ's church grow in effectiveness (and, often, in number) becomes an inner picture of a hoped-for future. As the clarity of this picture increases over time, it becomes more and more compelling. That is when the future bursts in upon the present of our ministries. Vision is about grasping God's future for the kingdom of God in our lives, times, and places.

The recognition that vision is a unique contribution of leadership is a relatively new phenomenon. But it has led to a burst of energy within the Christian church. Congregations and ministries have literally been reborn through the power of heaven-sent vision. On the other hand, other expressions of Christ's church have shrunk and collapsed without vision.

These devotions reflect on the realities of vision for Christian leaders. Among these realities are both possibility and frustration. Vision provokes decision-making. The leader must decide whether to follow and articulate the vision. Followers must assess both their willingness to pursue the vision and their level of support for it. This creates a dynamic interaction between Christian leaders and their constituencies. Throughout this dynamic process, the vision will be tested and clarified and, through the power of God's Spirit, taken further than the leader could have originally imagined.

As I've tried over the years to provide vision for my community of faith, I've both grown and been challenged by God's Word. I've learned that exercising leadership through vision casting is costly but essential. I share these devotions in the hope that they will encourage other leaders who either seek or already possess a vision for their ministries.

13 GOD'S FUTURE
Acts 10:9-23

"When I graduated from seminary, no one was talking about vision. Now it's all that I hear. I can tell you that I'm confused." The pastor was in his mid-thirties, bright, and energetic. His congregation was growing and, to most observers, he wouldn't have appeared stymied at all. But in this conversation with fellow pastors, his frustration was obvious.

"What I am afraid of is that my congregation will pay the price for my inability to understand, let alone develop, vision. How does it come, anyway?"

The pastor was right, of course. Most leaders, clergy or nonclergy, have not been trained to cast a vision. Yet vision casting is a critical leadership function. What are the elements of vision, and, once it comes, what do we do with it?

In Acts 10:9-23, Peter is surprised by a vision. The vision is clear and compelling, but Peter's response is revulsion, not elation. As he enters prayer, he sees a vision of a canopy descending from God's domain with every kind of non-kosher animal, insect, and reptile imaginable in it.

"Then a voice told him, 'Get up, Peter. Kill and eat.'

" 'Surely not, Lord!' Peter replied. 'I have never eaten anything impure or unclean.'

"The voice spoke to him a second time, 'Do not call anything impure that God has made clean.' This happened three times, and immediately the sheet was taken back to heaven" (Acts 10:13-16).

From this we learn that *vision is connected with prayer.* Peter was in prayer. His attention was focused on the things of God. Because he was attentive to God, he was available for a startling, new picture of God's provision. So vision emerges from our own discipleship.

VISION EMERGES FROM OUR OWN DISCIPLESHIP.

Then Peter's vision was very quickly confirmed by circumstances: "While Peter was wondering about the meaning of the vision, the men sent by Cornelius found out where Simon's house was and stopped at the gate. They called out, asking if Simon who was known as Peter was staying there. While Peter was still thinking about the vision, the Spirit said to him, 'Simon, three men are looking for you. So get up and go downstairs. Do not hesitate to go with them, for I have sent them' " (Acts 10:17-20).

Peter somehow knew that the vision wasn't about physical food, and he knew that God was saying something important to him. As Peter considered the vision and its meaning, he was presented with the opportunity to put the vision into action. He would be called to obey the Spirit in ways that violated all of his previously held convictions about Gentiles. The Spirit told him to go with Gentile servants, and he would eventually go into a Gentile house and worship with them. Under Mosaic law, these scandalous actions would have made him impure. Yet God called him to do these things as a matter of holy obedience.

This passage in Acts helped me work through a particularly difficult decision. We were planning to remodel our worship space when a parishioner approached me and said, "Pastor Mike, I don't think I can support the remodeling of our worship space because I don't believe in spending the church's money on bricks and mortar."

I struggled with that conversation for over two weeks. Was the remodeling the result of an *edifice complex*? Was it simply an extension of my pride or that of the congregation? I prayed a lot about it. I finally realized that the threadbare carpet, stained dark wood, and old furniture were impediments to outreach. (We actually preferred a certain photographer because his pictures of significant events in the worship space didn't reveal the carpet or stains!) While those who were used to it may not have cared about the tatters and stains, newcomers had to struggle to get past them.

That's when I discovered this wonderful passage in Acts. It seemed to me that God's vision is always about increasing access to those who are not yet included in grace. God's vision is always evangelical—it's about removing the barriers that keep people out. He removes barriers between Jews and Gentiles as well as between members and inquirers.

Oh, I'm sure that some still think that remodeling was both unnecessary and a sign of my personal spiritual arrogance. But Christian leaders learn that, sooner or later, anything we do can be misinterpreted or misunderstood. The real question is whether we've prayed and attended to God's will as we've discerned it.

Acts 11 describes the Jews' response to Peter's audacity. In explaining his actions, his defense was that he had no choice: "Who was I to think that I could oppose God?" (verse 17b). And, by the way, Paul makes it clear that this issue wasn't resolved for Peter until very late in his ministry. Even *Peter* didn't get it completely!

So God's vision will be tested, even after it has been confirmed. For Christian leaders, being given insight into God's vision is an invitation to courage. Will we have the courage to follow God's calling even though we know it will be misunderstood and challenged? This is the hard but necessary question for leaders with vision, because we will see what others have not seen and what we will not completely understand ourselves.

WILL WE HAVE THE COURAGE TO FOLLOW GOD'S CALLING EVEN THOUGH WE KNOW IT WILL BE MISUNDERSTOOD AND CHALLENGED?

LEADERSHIP PRAYER

O Holy Spirit, giver of vision, I pray that you will open my eyes and my heart to the future toward which you are calling me. Remind me that it is about your provision for others...not about me. And make the vision so compelling that when I feel like caving in and giving in to criticism or rejection, I'll rest in your strength. Amen.

TEAM *Matters*

Objective: for leaders to learn the three core principles for discerning God's vision for ministry.

Items needed: newsprint and colored pencils or markers.

CHALLENGE Have participants form pairs and designate one member A and the other member B. Ask the A's to imagine a welcoming church, a place where people who have never been to a church would feel at home. What type of building would it be? Instruct A's to imagine the rooms within the building and what might be happening in these rooms. While the A's are thinking about this, give each B a sheet of newsprint and a set of markers or pencils. After a few minutes, have the A's describe their churches to the B's as the B's illustrate them. A's may tell the B's about their churches, but only the B's may draw them. Give pairs five to ten minutes to complete this activity. One by one, have the B's share their drawings and oral descriptions of the churches with the rest of the group. Then ask the A's to comment on how well the B's interpreted their images.

READ & DISCUSS Have participants read Acts 10:9-23, then lead them through a discussion of the three aspects of vision that are described in the devotion: learning God's vision through prayer, the confirmation of God's vision through circumstances, and the evangelical nature of God's vision.

REFLECT Encourage participants to reflect upon the Scripture passage and the activity by pairing up and discussing the questions on page 77. Close the devotion by adapting the leadership prayer above to your group and setting.

1. Think about the church's image as described by the A member of your team.

- What made that church welcoming?
- How did the leader enable people to feel at home?
- Compare that ministry to your own. What is similar, and what is different?
- What can you do to break down the barriers that currently prevent people from hearing God's message? Make a list.

Pray about each item on the list in the next month, and listen to God's reply.

2. Do you currently have a vision for your ministry?

- Is this vision being confirmed by circumstances? If so, describe those circumstances. If not, what are the barriers?
- Do you think those barriers mean that God doesn't share this vision, or do you think they are evidence of the devil standing in your way?

As a leader, discerning the truth in this situation is hard. But we know that God always confirms visions that come from God. In the coming week, seek confirmation of your ministry's vision. Ask others. Look for signs that this vision is welcoming people into God's presence. And pray for God's discernment.

3. Is the vision of your ministry a safe goal or a bold evangelical vision? In other words, does it reach people already at church, or is it intended to stretch you to reach others?

- The second kind of vision requires courageous leadership. Are you putting your trust in your leadership or in God?
- How can you be instrumental in advancing God's vision in your setting?

Gather several others together once a week to pray specifically for the issues facing your ministry.

14 WHEN DOORS CLOSE
Acts 16:6-10

As a leader in Christ's church, the thing that frightens me more than anything is that I will go charging into the future, confident of God's leading, only to be stranded by my own arrogance.

Over the years, I have sometimes felt confident of the direction I had set for ministry. In some cases, circumstances caused the possibilities I was so sure of to evaporate. In others, when I shared my vision with those I trust, their patient and honest questioning led me to a very different conclusion. As hard as I worked to realize those visions, I just couldn't.

My natural response was to assume I'd done something wrong. But that may not have been the case at all. Sometimes God graciously blocks our efforts in order to open a better way.

In Acts 16:6-10, we discover that God blocked the well-intentioned plans of Paul and his company: "Paul and his companions traveled throughout the region of Phrygia and Galatia, *having been kept by the Holy Spirit from preaching the word in the province of Asia.* When they came to the border of Mysia, they tried to enter Bithynia, *but the Spirit of Jesus would not allow them to*" (verses 6-7).

> SOMETIMES GOD GRACIOUSLY BLOCKS OUR EFFORTS IN ORDER TO OPEN A BETTER WAY.

Paul and his companions tried to do what they believed God desired them to do, but God blocked them. This must have been so frustrating for them! They worked hard to preach in the province of Asia. God said no. Then God transformed their frustrations into a remarkable vision.

"So they passed by Mysia and went down to Troas. During the night Paul had a vision of a man of Macedonia standing and begging him, 'Come over to Macedonia and help us' " (Acts 16:8-9).

After blocking their efforts, God used their frustrations to create in them openness to a new vision. Their inability to move ahead with their original plans appears to have had nothing to do with any failure or inadequacy on their part. God blocked their efforts in order to give them an even greater mission opportunity!

This text suggests that frustration and confusion may open the door to mission. Paul's dream not only led him into a spectacular evangelical outreach, it created a team spirit within his group: "After Paul had seen the vision, *we* got ready at once to leave for Macedonia, concluding that God had called *us* to preach the gospel to them" (Acts 16:10).

I know that scholars conclude that this is when Luke may have joined Paul. The use of the first person plural (*we* and *us*) may demonstrate that. On the other hand, it seems to me that a compelling vision *creates community*. Paul's companions heard his dream and owned, for themselves, this call of God. We don't know if they were of differing opinions or variant convictions earlier, but we do know that Paul's dream solidified the direction and the team.

A COMPELLING VISION *CREATES COMMUNITY*.

The vision born out of frustration and seeming failure created an opportunity that would bless not only these missionaries, but countless other Christians of that time and since. Second Corinthians tells us that the generosity of the Macedonian Christians, their active love for others of faith, became legendary. Out of scarcity, God created abundance. And it all grew out of God's blocking Paul and his companions' plans.

Christian leaders can take heart in this remarkable protection of the Holy Spirit. The Holy Spirit will not only lead us, it will also prevent us from making great mistakes in order to open us to greater mission.

I have learned that when the best efforts of my ministry fail, perhaps it isn't about me. It may be that God has protected me and, in the process, opened my mind to new possibilities. Christian leaders can take heart in the knowledge that God will limit the harm we might do as well as the harm that comes to us. If we are willing, God just might make of our frustrations and perceived failures a great ministry.

LEADERSHIP PRAYER

O Holy Spirit, let me be open to new possibilities when you block my path. When things just don't seem to be going the right way for me, remind me of Paul and his companions. If you blocked them in order to open them to a new ministry possibility, then I know you may work like that in my life. Amen.

TEAM *Matters*

Objective: to remind leaders that when doors close, God may redirect them toward open windows.

Items needed: a penny for each participant, masking tape, and a whistle.

Preparation: Before this session, use masking tape to create a matrix on the floor of a large open area. Make one big square composed of sixty-four smaller squares (eight squares by eight squares). Make each square large enough for one person to stand in it. The object of the game you are designing is for participants to move through the matrix, from one side to the other, by stepping into one square at a time. Participants may move forward, to the right, and to the left, but not backward. With this in mind, design a path (which will be known only by you) that is the only correct way to travel through the matrix. Diagram your path so that you may refer to it during the activity, but be sure to keep it a secret.

CHALLENGE Have participants gather around the outside of the matrix, and give each participant a penny. Tell everyone, "Your penny is your resource. As a team, you want to keep as many resources as possible throughout this activity. The goal is to move, one at a time, through this matrix, stepping in one square at a time and moving forward, to the right, or to the left, but never backward. The catch is that there is only one correct pathway through the matrix, and this pathway is known only to me. If you step into a square that is not on the path, I'll blow a whistle, and you must retrace your steps *back* out of the matrix the same way as you came. Then someone else will try. We will continue until the path has been discovered; then everyone must move through the path. *The goal is to achieve this task in fifteen minutes, while losing the least number of pennies.* Pennies

Enriching THE EXPERIENCE

Read pages 25-76 of *Who Moved My Cheese?* by Spencer Johnson (copyright © 1998 G.P. Putnam's Sons) aloud to your group. As you read the story, post the signs in the room as they are placed on the wall in the story.

Ask participants to reflect on the story, especially in light of Acts 16:6-10. Ask:

- **What lesson emerged from this story for you?**
- **What does it tell us about our ministry?**
- **Which character in the story best describes our ministry? Why?**
- **What is the "cheese" in our work?**
- **Why might we get stuck or let obstacles prevent us from pursuing the cheese?**
- **How would you weave God into this story?**

TEAM *Matters*

(continued)

may be lost in one of three ways: (1) by talking. If anyone talks, either to another participant or to me, the team will lose a penny. (2) by not backing out of the matrix in the same way that you went in. (3) by entering the matrix when someone else is already in it. If two participants are anywhere in the matrix at the same time, the team will lose a penny. You will have fifteen minutes to accomplish your goal."

Answer any questions, repeat the goal, then begin.

DISCUSS Afterward, ask the group to reflect on the matrix activity. Ask the following questions aloud.

- How would you characterize this experience?
- What was frustrating about it?
- What went well?
- How did the team respond to mistakes, both in seeking the path and in breaking the rules?
- How did it feel to be the first one to step into the matrix?
- How did it feel to be the last?
- What did you learn from this activity?
- How does what you learned apply to your life in ministry?

READ & REFLECT Read aloud Acts 16:6-10. Encourage participants to reflect upon this Scripture and their own ministries by forming pairs and discussing the questions on page 82. Close in prayer. ■

Getting REAL

- Are there impediments to your ministry? What are they?
- Do you interpret them as doors closing?
- Are windows opening in your ministry? Do you recognize them as new possibilities?
- Is God planting God-sized visions in the hearts of our leaders?
- Do our visions require the work of God and a team?
- Do they compel others to join?
- Does our community operate from a perspective of scarcity or of abundance and hope?
- What resources has the Spirit planted in our community?
- What aspect of this process does our ministry need to focus on?
- What shall we, as a team, commit to pray for?

15 WHEN PEOPLE TURN AGAINST US

Luke 4:21-30

"I can't believe you did this," he said. Sitting in my office, this friend with whom I had worked and shared ministry, had a grievance. We had just made an administrative decision to eliminate a staff position. His friend was let go. The decision had cost me hours of lost sleep and driven me to my knees. In the end, all of us on the leadership team knew that it had to be done.

Having spent time with the person who had lost his job, this friend was now in my office. Anger flashed in his eyes. Suspicion lurked in his heart. "No matter what you say, I know this is about power. Your great temptation is power, and now you've misused it. Don't glorify it with holy language or prayer. It's just wrong."

The conversation didn't last much longer. I had lost his friendship. Worse, I feared he would share his judgment of me with others. Because the matter was confidential, I couldn't tell him the details that had made the decision necessary. So I prayed. I trusted the judgment of the leadership team and dared to believe that God would honor our prayerful, clear-eyed evaluation and action.

Few conflicts are more painful than those surrounding vision. They are painful because most of us do not recognize that they are about vision so we personalize them. The events that led to the elimination of that staff position included a series of discussions and conflicts with that person about our ministry's direction. In fact, it was only as I was reading Luke 4:21-30 that I realized we were engaged in a conflict of vision—just as Jesus was in this text.

When our Lord spoke to the people in the synagogue in Nazareth, their first response was warm and enthusiastic: "All spoke well of him and were amazed at the gracious words that came from his lips. 'Isn't this Joseph's son?' they asked" (Luke 4:22).

Jesus then began to share his vision for his ministry. He had not been sent to be owned by them. Their limited and selfish designs for him would be exposed. His ministry was not about them but about the expanding, inclusive will of God. This is the redeeming will that led Elijah to Zarephath and a widow's need. This is the same reaching out by God that healed a Gentile warrior through the prophet Elisha. Now Jesus was called to extend the kingdom of God beyond the confines of his community and its members' desires and imaginations.

The response of his friends to this great vision was immediate. "All the people in the synagogue were furious when they heard this. They got up, drove him out of the town, and took him to the brow of the hill on which the town was built, in order to throw him down the cliff. But he walked right through the crowd and went on his way" (Luke 4:28-30).

Christian leaders are no freer from such rejection than our Lord was. This fact doesn't make rejection less painful. But it can help us understand and accept it as the necessary consequence of a vision for ministry that is the call of God.

THE VISION THAT GOD GIVES WILL BE TESTED.

Jesus models for us a number of spiritual truths in this text. The first is that the vision that God gives will be tested. That test will often include the misunderstandings and judgments of those who have been our friends. When friends reject us, as they did our Lord, it can be because our vision goes further or is different from theirs. Their understanding of our ministries, calls, and passions is limited. Such conflicts test our commitment and clarity of vision. Jesus held fast. If our vision is for a ministry that is inspired by God, we, too, are called to hold fast.

Second, Jesus shows us that choosing our vision may provoke others to make choices about us. In Nazareth, the choice of those in the synagogue was dramatic. They moved from embracing the Savior to intending to murder him. My friend made a clear choice about our friendship. (I am thankful that he later reconsidered his choice.) Leaders understand that sometimes decisions must be made that we would rather avoid and cannot discuss freely. And, even if we can discuss our reasons, there are some decisions that others will simply not accept. If these decisions are surrounded by prayer and helpful conversations with trusted colleagues and leaders and held up to the mirror of our vision, we enter the conflict with the confidence of the Holy Spirit.

Third, this text demonstrates that the power of the vision will lead us through the conflict. At the brow of the hill, Jesus simply *walked right through the crowd*. The call of God expressed in our vision has great power to encourage and empower Christian leaders to act and persist through the heat of conflict and rejection—even rejection by friends.

There are few conflicts within the church that are not resolvable through compromise, but in conflicts of vision, there is no middle ground. Either one vision or another will be chosen. In this text, the Lord models the faithful pursuit of a vision. For you and me, this is not as easy as it appears to have been for Jesus. The hurt and inner struggle I experienced didn't end with the decision or with that conversation. I returned to the leadership team again and again to evaluate the process and the decisions. Each time I was encouraged that we had done the right thing.

Was it worth it? Yes. I know that it will not be the last time conflicts will require this kind of action. I pray that next time I'll be better able to test the conflict and discern how much is about vision and how much is about me. The Savior always knew what he was about. As leaders, let us always examine ourselves and our actions in the light of his life and Word.

LEADERSHIP PRAYER

Lord Jesus, empower me to face conflict and not run from it. Forgive me when the conflict is about me. Encourage me when it comes because I am striving to faithfully pursue your vision. Amen.

TEAM *Matters*

Objective: for leaders to understand that visions will be tested and to learn what to do during those times.

Items needed: a volleyball or basketball for each participant and a room big enough to move around in.

CHALLENGE Give each participant a ball. Have everyone find a spot on the floor away from others, sit down, and place the ball between his or her knees. Then, without letting his or her hands touch the ground or the ball, have each participant try to stand up, keeping the ball between his or her knees.

Allow a few minutes for participants to struggle to do this. Then have them try again, but this time allow them to lean, back to back, against other participants. See if this "added resource" makes the process easier.

Enriching THE EXPERIENCE

If time allows, listen to the song "Above All" by Lenny LeBlanc and Paul Baloche, which may be found on Michael W. Smith's *Worship* CD. As you listen to this song, remember the price Jesus was willing to pay to accomplish the vision set before him by God. Just as God had a hand on Jesus the day he was rejected in Nazareth, God was with him throughout his journey, even through his death on the cross.

As a group, make a pledge to be resources for one another during times of conflict. Articulate what that means for *your* group.

DISCUSS & REFLECT Invite participants to discuss this experience and to identify themes that emerged from it. Tell everyone that today's devotion is about a time people turned against Jesus. Read Luke 4:21-30 aloud, then distribute the questions on page 86. Allow time for participants to work by themselves, in pairs, or as a group, choosing the method that best fits your setting.

Getting REAL

1. Reflect on times you've relied on others' opinions to shape your work. Was their input helpful or harmful?

- Did the information you gained from others help shape your ideas, and if so, in what ways?
- Did the information you gained sidetrack you from your work? If so, what was the result?
- What role did God play during those times?
- How did you invite God into the process?
- What vision or plan are you currently struggling with?
- What are others saying to you?
- How are you bringing God into the situation?

This week, spend ten minutes each day bringing this situation before God, then see what happens.

2. Think about a time people turned against you because of a leadership decision you made.

- What were the circumstances?
- Did you make the decision alone or with others?
- How were you treated by those who disagreed with the decision?
- What was the personal cost of the decision?
- What happened to you spiritually during that time?
- If someone who was going through a similar situation came to you now, what advice would you give that person?

3. Getting through conflict is easier when we're focused on God.

- What methods do you use to help you focus on God?
- Cite Scripture passages that would be helpful during such a time.
- What price are you willing to pay to pursue God's vision? A loss of friends? A few difficult conversations? Your spiritual health? Your family or marriage? The respect of those you love?

16 ASKING THE RIGHT QUESTION

Luke 18:35-43

I have been told that when I'm in a hurry, I have a certain way of walking that fairly screams, "Don't interrupt me; I'm on a mission!" I'm sure I was walking that way as I left our worship center.

"Pastor Mike! Pastor Mike!" I heard a young voice call. I quickly judged that the voice was far enough behind me that I could ignore it. Continuing across the parking lot, I suddenly tripped and nearly fell. I caught myself and, in the process, steadied a five-year-old child I hadn't even noticed. Now I looked into two of the most beautiful brown eyes I had ever seen. There were tears in her eyes as she looked up at me and said, "Pastor Mike, I almost missed you," and I thought, "No, I almost missed *you*."

I stopped, knelt down, and asked, "Was that you calling me?" Then we had the most marvelous conversation about that morning's children's sermon. This child of God told me about her love of Jesus and of me! And all my reasons for hurrying were forgotten as I stilled my spirit to hear what this child had to tell me.

One of the more remarkable aspects of our Lord's ministry was his ability to stop and pay attention to others. In Luke 18:35-43, Jesus had turned to go to Jerusalem. He knew what was in store for him, and his focus was crystal clear. He shared his knowledge and resolve with the disciples, but the disciples didn't understand any of it. As Jesus passed through Jericho, on the way to Jerusalem, a blind man learned who was passing by and cried out to him, "Jesus, Son of David, have mercy on me!" (Luke 18:38).

This is when it gets interesting. I don't know if Jesus was walking one of "those walks" or not. What seems clear is that those around him didn't want him to be interrupted, so they told the blind man to be quiet. But he persisted and was rewarded when Jesus stopped and asked that the blind man be brought to him. And when the blind man stood before the Savior, Jesus asked a most remarkable question: "What do you want me to do for you?" (Luke 18:41).

I am struck by the question because it seems so unnecessary. After all, the man's blindness would have been obvious. Why ask the question?

We leaders often assume that we understand the need before us. We are used to making decisions after assessing, at times very quickly, situations. Jesus didn't do that.

JESUS TOOK THE TIME TO STOP AND ASK THE RIGHT QUESTION.

Even when he was so clearly focused on his goal, he took the time to stop and ask the right question. The right question reveals the real need. That is what happened in this text. That is what I experienced in that brief but significant encounter with that little girl.

There are many enemies of asking the right question, but two stand out. The first is overcommitment. We find ourselves rushing from one thing to the next. That was my situation when I almost missed a wonderful opportunity to hear a little girl witness to me. It's hard to stop in the midst of our busy-ness, but stopping is essential for us to ask the right question.

Jesus stopped. He stood still long enough to invite the blind man forward and to take him seriously. Jesus honored that man with his attention, and the right question emerged as a result.

A second enemy of asking the right question is listening to others. Jesus wasn't swayed by the wisdom of the crowd. Apparently, those around our Lord judged that the blind man was not worthy of the Savior's time and attention.

As leaders, there will be those around us who will want to protect our time and energies. We ought to thank God for them and their efforts on our behalf. But the truth is that sometimes we miss the gifts God would send our way. We miss the opportunity to hear that witness or receive the word of correction we need. How can we discern this? Perhaps the best way is to simply listen to that small voice within us that often is the voice of the Spirit. When the Spirit whispers that we ought to stop and pay attention, let's heed that voice—no matter what those around us may be saying.

I have a wonderful helper in my administrative assistant, Lee. One of the things that I value so highly about our partnership is that, occasionally, she will say to me, "This is someone you need to see." It stops me in my tracks. I pay attention, and we almost always schedule the appointment.

Christian leaders need to be reminded often to slow down and pay attention. Sometimes the Holy Spirit tackles us and seizes our attention, just as that little girl did in the parking lot. More often than not, however, we need those we trust to tell us. If we are willing, we will learn to stand still before others and honor them by asking the right question. Remarkably, the right question is often the obvious one. The answer, however, is an open door to the miracles of God.

LEADERSHIP PRAYER

Lord Jesus, teach me to ask the right questions in my ministry, just as you stopped in Jericho and asked the right question of the blind man. Forgive me when I act on the assumption that I already know what is needed. Slow me down, and, when necessary, send the Holy Spirit to tackle me! Amen.

TEAM *Matters*

OBJECTIVE: for leaders to discover that asking the right questions in leadership requires them to hear God's voice.

ITEMS NEEDED: paper and pencils for each participant, a CD player and a CD of raucous music, a TV, a clock with a loud "tick tock," a cell phone, and any other noisemakers you can find.

PREPARATION: Consider meeting in a different room from where your group usually meets, such as the youth room, copy room, or boiler room. Before this session, arrange to have someone call you on your cell phone repeatedly during the meeting.

PREPARE Before everyone arrives, create an atmosphere filled with noise! Start the CD of raucous music, and turn up the volume. Turn the TV to a channel with only "snow" showing, and turn up the volume. Set the loud clock nearby. When it's time to begin the meeting, allow the noises to continue. As you go, make mental notes of the participants' responses.

CHALLENGE Over the noise, invite the group to take part in a lesson about asking the right questions. Begin with prayer, then ask participants to list ten questions they think are important to leaders in ministry. Do your best to keep the noise level high for as long as possible. As the noises become more irritating, turn them off one by one.

REACT When you've achieved silence, wait for comments about the distractions, and encourage participants to describe their reactions to the noise. Then invite them to make a second list, this time of things that get in the way of discovering their ministries' real needs.

PRAY & DISCUSS After they complete the second list, ask them to move to a new environment. Choose a quiet space such as a chapel or counseling room. Once everyone is settled, open again with prayer. Ask everyone to find a partner with whom to share one or two items from each list. Ask pairs to read Luke 13:35-43 aloud together, then encourage them to reflect upon this Scripture and the activity by discussing the questions on page 90. ■

Enriching THE EXPERIENCE

Close your time together with a brief worship time. Listen to or sing "Open the Eyes of My Heart" by Paul Baloche, which may be found on Michael W. Smith's *Worship* CD. Encourage participants to use this quiet time to confess the sins that prevent them from hearing God's voice and to then simply listen to God's voice. After the song, sit in silence for a time, then close in prayer.

Getting REAL

1. How did you respond to the first part of this activity?

- What emotions did it stir within you?
- When have you felt that way before?
- These noises are common in the world around us. What, if anything, made hearing them today different?
- What noises surround you daily? Can you escape them?

This week, make a commitment to God to spend five to ten minutes each day in total silence, just being with God—no reading, no music, just quiet time alone with God.

2. Have you heard God's voice in your life?

- How did you know it was God's?
- When have you heard God through other people?
- What was the result of those experiences?
- Has God ever been revealed to you through a small voice inside you? Why did you think the voice was God's?
- What came of that idea or words?
- Has hearing God's voice ever helped you ask a "right" question? What happened?
- How was God revealed in that situation? Was glory given to God?

In the coming month, pay attention to God's voice. Note the times God speaks to you as well as the results.

3. The crowd wanted to shoo away the blind man, but Jesus stopped and talked with him anyway.

- Who does our world discard?
- How would Jesus respond to people who have been discarded by society?
- If the blind man was worthy of Jesus' time, what does that say about who is worthy of our time?
- What right question does this raise in your life? in your ministry?

In the next couple of days, take time to notice those around you who the world discards. Then ask God what right question that raises for your ministry.

17 THE AIM OF LEARNING

1 Timothy 1:3-7

"He's so heavenly minded that he's no earthly good."

As I was growing up, I used to hear this saying about some Christians. The idea was that their religion was so spiritual that it had little or no impact on the real world. They could talk about God, but they never put their faith in God to work for the sake of others.

Paul's vision for ministry is practical. In his first letter to Timothy, he urged Timothy to hold fast to the practical outcome of Christian teaching and to remember that the aim of learning is love. This love "comes from a pure heart and a good conscience and a sincere faith" (1 Timothy 1:5b). Its opposite is the kind of teaching or learning that promotes controversy or "meaningless talk" (1 Timothy 1:6b).

One of the great threats to the early church was Gnosticism. This was a form of religion that promoted knowledge (the term is derived from the Greek word *gnosis*, which means *knowledge*) as the means to salvation. This special knowledge was available to only a select few who *got it.* Often filled with speculations about levels of spiritual beings and an understanding of God that denied the Incarnation, Gnosticism divided the Christian community into sects of the learned. The aim of their learning was a holy knowledge that was kept from others. Such a concept would naturally produce controversy as one idea was held as superior to another. Truly, such persons were "so heavenly minded that they were of no earthly good." And Paul knew that. He urged Timothy to hold all teaching accountable to that love that builds up the body of Christ. Paul was so intent on this that he used a threefold repetition of thought in his language: "pure heart," "good conscience," and "sincere faith."

ONE OF THE MAJOR REASONS PEOPLE REMAIN OUTSIDE THE CHURCH IS THEIR PERCEPTION THAT CHRISTIANS FIGHT AMONG THEMSELVES TOO MUCH.

I read that one of the major reasons people remain outside the church is their perception that Christians fight among themselves too much. I can believe it. We are often so determined that our opinions are the only right way of thinking that we criticize and demean others of faith who disagree with us. People outside the church don't see the issues so much as the contrariness of the controversy. Consequently the body of Christ is damaged.

One of the unconfessed sins of the church is pastoral jealousy. I struggled with jealousy when a church of a different denomination was growing in the community I was serving and my church was stuck on a plateau. Instead of trying to learn from that church, I talked about its flawed teaching. This may have made me feel a bit better, but our congregation didn't turn around until my attitude changed.

ONE OF THE UNCONFESSED SINS OF THE CHURCH IS PASTORAL JEALOUSY.

I believe that the Spirit of God is moving in our time to renew the church in keeping with this teaching of Paul. Increasingly, I hear Christian leaders of many denominations talking about a "kingdom mentality," which urges us to move beyond interchurch competition to view our work as complementary. We are all serving the same Savior and seeking to build God's kingdom on earth. Pastoral jealousy is set aside. We hold our own opinions and interpretations of doctrine and Scripture but do not want to express them in ways that compromise the effective preaching of the gospel. I think we are relearning that the aim of our knowledge is not division but love.

In 1 Timothy 1:3-7, Christian leaders are invited to align their vision of the purpose of theology and biblical knowledge with Paul's. As a young seminary graduate, I thought my theology was second to none. My understanding of the Bible was clear, and I held to it with conviction. Unfortunately, this arrogance was not tempered by a sensitivity to the impact harsh words could have on the lives of others. As Paul teaches elsewhere, all things are lawful. Not all things are helpful. Even if I was right in my interpretation of this or that biblical or theological matter, it wasn't always necessary or helpful to say it.

Christian leaders are called to a higher goal than just being right or knowledgeable. The aim is love, an active building up of the faith of others. When the truth is debated to that end, even disagreements can be positive. Our vision is subject to our Lord's vision of the kingdom of God. That is what Paul told Timothy to remember and to teach—as well as hold others accountable to.

When I think of some of the theological arguments in which I engaged, I can only chuckle and trust that the Savior has more patience with me than I had with others. With this forgiveness as a foundation, I can seek to learn from other Christian leaders and grow as a laborer in God's realm. There is a wonderful freedom in this. The burden of being right is lifted, and I can accept the yoke of Christ's love in its place.

LEADERSHIP PRAYER

O Holy Spirit, when I am tempted to argue with others about doctrine or even the Word of God, help me to discern if the debate is necessary and helpful. I want to be so heavenly minded that my earthly good is multiplied over and over in the lives of others. And I would not want to provide any with an excuse to turn from your work in Christ's church. Remind me, again and again, that the true aim of my learning is love. Amen.

TEAM *Matters*

Objective: to remind leaders that the aim of learning is love that builds up the body of Christ.

Items needed: *All I Really Need to Know I Learned in Kindergarten*, a book by Robert Fulghum and published by Ivy Books, copyright © 1988; index cards; a pen; and, for each participant, paper and a pencil.

Preparation: Before the session, write the words of 1 Timothy 1:5 on index cards, one card for each participant.

CHALLENGE Read aloud pages 4 and 5 of *All I Really Need to Know I Learned in Kindergarten*. The section begins "Share everything" and ends "...the biggest word of all—LOOK." Then have participants write their own versions of this list under the title "All I Really Need to Know About My Faith I Learned in Sunday School." Have participants share their lists with the group.

READ & REFLECT Read 1 Timothy 1:3-7 aloud. Then ask participants to consider the questions on page 94. You may wish to have them work through the questions by themselves or in groups of two or three.

PRAY Give everyone a card with the words of 1 Timothy 1:5 written on it, then close in prayer. ■

Getting REAL

1. Reread your list titled "All I Really Need to Know About My Faith I Learned in Sunday School."

- How would your life be different if you lived according to those principles?
- How would your teaching, preaching, or leading be different if you focused on those principles?
- Who are some people who model this life?

Post your list in your office or somewhere at home so that you will see it each day. Let it remind you to live the basics of your faith in the coming week.

2. What do you have to unlearn?

- What bad habits have you allowed to seep into your faith life?
- What should you replace these bad habits with?
- " 'Everything is permissible for me'—but not everything is beneficial" (1 Corinthians 6:12). What does this verse mean to you?
- When have you used the first part of this verse as an excuse for doing something, forgetting about the second part?
- What standard do you use to decide what is beneficial for your life?
- Can love of yourself and others be that standard?

Use 1 Corinthians 6:12 as part of your prayer time each day this week. Ask God to guide you in making choices that are not only permissible but also beneficial to you and your faith.

3. Hold up your vision to the test of love found in 1 Timothy 1:3-7. How does it fare?

- Does your vision strive toward building a community that exercises this type of love?
- Are you missing something? What?
- What parts of your vision reflect this loving community?

18 MAKING THE UNKNOWN KNOWN

Acts 17:22-31

One day I was interviewing a prospective staff member at Prince of Peace. As senior pastor, one of my responsibilities is to embody and articulate the culture that God has called our church to foster. So I was meeting with this person to talk about our practices of faith, the "marks of discipleship." I had just begun to tell her that these marks are not about perfection, but about growing, when she interrupted me.

"I have so much to be thankful for. I have discovered that the marks of discipleship have opened me to a wonderful call of God. It's not about meeting a standard of faith that is beyond me. It's really about growing strong in Jesus," she said. "I was talking with members of my neighborhood Bible study group, and we all have found that the more Christian we become, the less we need to judge anyone else. The more outside of the faith we are, the more we worry about other Christians judging us. I just hope that the faith I have grown into can be shared with people who don't know Jesus."

THE MORE CHRISTIAN WE BECOME, THE LESS WE NEED TO JUDGE ANYONE ELSE.

I was once again humbled by the privilege of Christian leadership. The wonder of our calling is that the Lord has invited us to share a vision of faith with those who are seeking him. This person's remarkable faith journey began with a lifestyle without faith. After suffering a personal failure, she turned to Jesus and, in so doing, began to rebuild her life. She had heard the message of a forgiving God who gives us as many second chances as we need to "get it right." This is the God that she had longed for, the God she had not known except in the deepest parts of herself. The privilege of Christian leadership is to make the unknown known.

In Acts 17:22-31, Paul models this opportunity for us. He begins where his hearers are. "Paul then stood up in the meeting of the Areopagus and said: 'Men of Athens! I see that in every way you are very religious. For as I walked around and looked carefully at your objects of worship, I even found an altar with this inscription: to an unknown god. Now what you worship as something unknown I am going to proclaim to you' " (Acts 17:22-23). Making the unknown known in Jesus Christ is the call of Christian leadership.

We know that this is not always easy, nor is it always immediately successful. Paul's message of the resurrection of Jesus was met with mixed reactions. Some scoffed. Some wanted to hear more. And Luke tells us that "a few men became followers of Paul and believed" (Acts 17:34a). That means, of course, that many didn't believe. But that ought not discourage us. For we know that Athens would later become the center of a great Christian witness, the witness of the Greek Orthodox church. Paul was sowing the seeds of faith; he wouldn't see the harvest, but history would.

SPIRITUAL LONGING IS PRESENT IN ALL PEOPLE.

We don't know who turned Paul's witness into a movement of the Holy Spirit that formed a great religious tradition. But we do know that Paul was faithful to his calling to make the unknown known in the risen one, Jesus Christ.

The woman whose interview I described earlier ultimately became a member of our staff. She is one of those saints who received the witness of the church. Through that witness, the unknown God for whom she longed became known to her in Jesus Christ. Now she strives to share this same good news with children and their parents.

The vision for our ministry is not that we will tell everyone. Rather, it is that God will use our witness, like Paul's, to raise up others who will share the good news of Jesus in compelling ways. This young woman will speak to another generation of inquirers. The seeds of the Word will bear fruit beyond measure through her work.

Paul understood the inner spiritual hunger that the gospel alone can satisfy. He said, "The God who made the world and everything in it is the Lord of heaven and earth and does not live in temples built by hands...and he determined the times set for them [humankind] and the exact places where they should live. God did this so that men would seek him and perhaps reach out for him and find him, though he is not far from each one of us" (Acts 17:24, 26b-27). According to Paul, God works within every human heart, whether we know God or not. This working is expressed as a spiritual longing. The task of Christian leaders is to identify this inner longing and direct it toward the God made known in Jesus of Nazareth. Once people make that connection, they will tell others.

Christian leaders are rarely the evangelists of our time. The evangelists are those who, like this woman, speak of the grace of Jesus to those who are outside the institutional church. They have opportunities to speak to persons with whom most Christian leaders will never converse. As Christian leaders share, we are called to equip others to share. This multiplies the grace of God and spreads the gospel. But make no mistake about it—spiritual longing is present in all people.

Vision is like that. Once the leader shares it, it no longer belongs to him or her. Others will hear, receive, and own that vision. They will take it places the leader had never imagined. After Paul's speech in Athens, I doubt he had any inkling of the church that would rise from his failed attempt to evangelize the Greeks. But with the hindsight of history, we can see it clearly.

Christian leaders learn from this that when we share the good news of Jesus, the Holy Spirit makes more of it than we could ever plan or anticipate. This knowledge allows us to share the gospel with confidence.

Are you willing to trust God to make of your vision more than you ever could? If so, don't be surprised when others speak of your sharing as a gift that has become their very own witness.

LEADERSHIP PRAYER

Lord Jesus, make of my sharing whatever you desire. I ask only that you increase my faith so that, even when I feel I have failed, I will trust you to be at work to harvest an abundance of spiritual fruit. Let me boldly declare your goodness and then trust you with the outcome. Amen.

TEAM *Matters*

Objective: to remind leaders that their lives are a living witness and to challenge them to evaluate that witness.

Items needed: a dictionary and eight to ten pictures of recognizable places that give witness to certain events or experiences, such as an Olympic stadium (which gives witness to athletic excellence and unity among nations). Other ideas include Disney World, the White House, a hospital, and a church.

CHALLENGE Begin by reading a dictionary's definition of the word *witness* ("to testify to" or "one that gives evidence" or "public affirmation of by word or example"). Show the group the pictures, one by one. After each, ask participants to identify the picture and describe what it witnesses to the world.

SHARE Tell about a time someone was a witness to you, then invite participants to share stories about people who have been witnesses to them. Read Acts 17:22-31 aloud. Ask participants to think about their own witness as Christian leaders.

REFLECT Encourage everyone to reflect upon this Scripture by responding to the questions on page 98, either in writing or orally in groups of two or three. ■

1. Does your witness cause others to seek God?

- Do your actions give witness to God? What about your heart?
- How has God transformed your life? Are you able to share that story with others?
- Are you living as a transformed person still today?

Our lives, once they intersect with God's unconditional love, can become the most powerful witness. If you have not shared your faith story with someone, do so this week.

2. What earthly things have become the focus of your life?

- What are the "statues" in your life? What do they represent?
- Have rituals of faith replaced your efforts to seek God with all your heart?
- Does your life indicate that "doing church" is more important than transforming people's hearts?
- What is the focus of your ministry?
- Does your witness remain on the surface when people are yearning to go deeper in their spiritual walk?
- Does the vision of your ministry capture people's desire to deepen their faith?

Spend time reviewing the work of your ministry in light of these questions, then redirect your ministry as needed.

3. How well do you equip others to share their faith stories?

- Are you creating opportunities for people to talk about the transformation that is underway in their lives?
- What would happen if you allowed time for these opportunities in your ministry?
- When have you allowed for this kind of sharing? What happened?
- What would it take to gain momentum in this area?

Take time this week to listen to others' stories of transformation. Thank God for these witnesses of faith. Pray for opportunities for such sharing in your ministry.

Section Four

RAISING UP LEADERS AROUND YOU

The church in the United States faces a crisis of leadership. This is evidenced both by leaders who are struggling to renew their energy for ministry and by a growing shortage of church leaders. Raising up leaders around us is an essential task for Christian leaders. How do we do it? What are the blessings and challenges of identifying, developing, and turning loose other leaders? More important, what are some of the spiritual truths that God's Word has to share with us about this critical task?

Through these devotions, I invite you to share some of what I've learned as I've tried to raise up other leaders over the years. In some of the devotions, my mistakes are evident. In others, I reveal some risks of sharing ministry. But beneath each devotion is the conviction that sharing leadership is the best way to lead. Leaders who discover the joy of celebrating the successes of the leaders around them know its power to renew them. Leaders who can help others learn from failures are reminded of how God truly can make blessings out of our struggles.

When we dare to raise up leaders around us, we are welcomed into the hard but rewarding work of identifying and equipping others to excel. Sometimes that will mean letting them go. Other times, it will mean stepping back and lifting them above ourselves. My experience is that every Christian leader has a "John the Baptist calling" that requires us to eventually point to another and say, "This person must increase while I decrease." The reward is knowing that we have contributed to the church of God's future.

19 RAISE THEM UP
Acts 6:1-7

My friend had an appointment with a potential leader in one of his key small groups. They met in her office, and she said, "I'm not sure what you expect of me. I know that you want me to lead this group and you've provided materials for me to do that. But, beyond getting the people together and having some discussion, I don't know what you expect me to do." She paused and, perhaps seeing the look of bewilderment on his face, continued, "In my work, we talk about what we hope will be accomplished. So that's what I need to know from you. When all is said and done, what do you really want me to accomplish? And what difference will that make in how our church does its work?"

My friend told me this was one of the most enlightening, albeit uncomfortable, conversations he'd ever had. This was his first encounter with a person who viewed her efforts within the context of the whole church. She wanted to know how her service would advance the mission of his congregation. He told me that, on the one hand, he was flattered that she was asking the questions he was constantly preaching about. On the other hand, he didn't know how to answer her. Even though he told me later that he couldn't remember how he had responded, she agreed to his position. And her small group grew. Soon those in the group became a core of service for his church.

THE TWELVE KNEW THAT THEIR JOB WAS NOT TO DO EVERYTHING THAT NEEDED TO BE DONE.

Opportunity is born out of need. In Acts 6:1-7 we read of the first "church fight." The Greek widows were not being cared for adequately in the Jerusalem church. The Twelve gathered all the disciples and presented a plan. The congregation was to raise up leaders who would see to the fair distribution of food to all.

In this text there are three key lessons for leaders. The first is that the Twelve knew that their job was not to do everything that needed to be done: "So the Twelve gathered all the disciples together and said, 'It would not be right for us to neglect the ministry of the word of God in order to wait on tables' " (Acts 6:2). Because they knew their own work, they knew their limitations. Even as they articulated those limitations, though, they also acknowledged the real need confronting them.

That leads to the second lesson: The Twelve faced the issue head on. There is no excuse-making here. Instead, because they knew that they couldn't do it all, they looked to others for help.

In my friend's conversation with that emerging leader, he talked of his need for her help. He couldn't do all that needed to be done. His plate was full, and he was looking for someone else of Christian character and mature faith to lead this key small group.

That is the third key lesson in this text: The Twelve articulated not only what the new leaders would do but also what their qualifications would be. "Brothers, choose seven men from among you who are known to be full of the Spirit and wisdom. We will turn this responsibility over to them" (Acts 6:3).

Early in my ministry, I heard a respected pastor lament the shortage of teachers in his Sunday school. He said that all he was looking for were a few live bodies. Anyone who breathed was eligible! All of us sympathized at the time. Now, however, I know how we minimize our assessment of the time and energy we ask of those who serve in the church. The Twelve had no such illusions. They made it clear: These had to be mature people of faith who were also noted for their wisdom. Just breathing wouldn't do!

WE MINIMIZE OUR ASSESSMENT OF THE TIME AND ENERGY WE ASK OF THOSE WHO SERVE IN THE CHURCH.

I don't know the process used in this first-century Christian community to identify these leaders. I do know that whatever it was, it worked. We read about Stephen, the passionate witness of the faith who became our first martyr. We also read about Philip, whose witness established the great Ethiopian Christian church that still stands today. There is no reason to suspect that the other five were any less passionate followers of Jesus.

The disciples publicly entrusted great responsibility to seven men who were still under the spiritual instruction of the Twelve. The outcome is described in Acts 6:7: "So the word of God spread. The number of disciples in Jerusalem increased rapidly, and a large number of priests became obedient to the faith."

God blesses our honest efforts to raise up leaders. My friend shared with joy the success and learning that sprang from that conversation. It has shaped his approach to enlisting others in leadership.

I believe one of the great, yet largely unacknowledged, responsibilities of leaders is to identify and raise up other leaders. The great crisis the church in our time faces is a crisis of leadership. The call to lead is the call to replicate ourselves in the unique lives and service of others...just as the Twelve did.

LEADERSHIP PRAYER

O Lord of leaders, empower me to identify the leaders you have sent to me. Then, by the power of your Holy Spirit, give me boldness in speaking with them and entrusting your ministry to them. I ask this not only for my sake but also for the sake of your kingdom. Amen.

TEAM *Matters*

Objective: for leaders to understand the need for raising up other leaders and to learn how to identify them.

Items needed: paper and a pencil for each participant.

CHALLENGE Give everyone a sheet of paper and a pencil. Ask participants to think of an area of ministry in which they are currently working. Then ask them to identify a specific issue that ministry has faced. For example, perhaps the Sunday school needed to recruit three teachers or the stewardship committee needed to raise $10,000 for a new parking lot. After everyone has identified a need, tell him or her to double the problem. So, for example, if the Sunday school at first needed three teachers, it now needs six. Ask participants how they are feeling. Is anyone anxious? Ask everyone to write the names of two or three people who might be able to help with the need. Stipulate that the names must be of people who are not already on the person's team.

Now double the problem again. So, if at first the Sunday school needed three teachers, it now needs twelve. Ask everyone to add four or five names to the list of potential helpers. Check in with the participants. Are they anxious yet? Give everyone a few minutes to think of more names. This will be a struggle for most; if it's not, double the need again.

DISCUSS Then ask the following questions of the group at large.

- As the activity progressed, how did the pressure change?
- Did the task become overwhelming at some point? If so, how would you describe your reaction? If not, at what point would it have become overwhelming?
- Imagine that you had faced this problem in reality. Once you could think of no more names, what method would you have used to identify more people?
- Is there a point at which you simply would have quit?
- What would have caused you to quit?
- What would have made the effort worth pursuing?

IMAGINE Now ask participants to imagine that they are Christians living in the time right after Pentecost. Encourage them to imagine the apostles preaching about the resurrected Christ and the response of the people who heard and believed this good news. Tell them that as the number of Christians grew, so also did their needs. Read aloud Acts 6:1-7, then ask participants to form groups of two or three in which to discuss the questions on page 103. ■

Getting REAL

1. Do you know your limits?

- What do you do when you get close to exceeding limits?
- Is it easy or hard for you to hand work over to someone else?
- Would you have been as open to adding new leaders as the early apostles were? Why or why not?
- What would have happened if this team had remained "in charge" and let the physical limitations of twelve people determine its ministry capacity?
- What is limiting your ministry?
- What step of faith do you need to take to release the potential of God's work in your ministry?

Take time this week to identify your ministry's real needs and your limitations in meeting those needs.

2. What makes a good leader?

- How did the apostles identify new leaders?
- Can you identify people with leadership potential?
- How do you recruit other leaders?
- How intentional is your ministry in reproducing its leadership?
- What support are you ready to give emerging leaders?
- What system or structure does your ministry have in place for supporting new leaders? Do emerging leaders know of this support system?
- Do leaders know what is expected of them and the outcome you are hoping their efforts will produce? Are the leaders held accountable?
- Do you feel your ministry expects too much or too little of its leaders?
- How can these expectations be adjusted?

If this is an area in your ministry that needs attention, create a team of people with a passion for leadership development. Ask them to evaluate the current process and make suggestions for improvement.

20 ACCEPT THEIR QUESTIONS

John 1:43-51

I have a new goal in life. I want to drive my car as if I'm not impatiently trying to get somewhere. This isn't easy for me. I am a repentant *rush-aholic*. I am addicted to hurrying when I get behind the wheel of an automobile. It doesn't matter if I've left myself plenty of time to reach my destination. As soon as I come up behind someone going much more slowly than I, my pulse begins to race. Or if someone cuts in front of me, causing me to slow considerably, I am sorely tempted to bear down on him in punitive tailgating. I'm not proud of it. I am, as I just said, repentant.

The cause of my repentance? I'd like to say that this change is the result of prayer or a holy insight. It's not. It happened because I married a truth-teller. My wife has a habit of getting at the truth of my character in subtle but revealing ways. Recently she simply asked, "Why are you driving so fast? We have more than enough time to get where we're going. Wouldn't you feel better if you slowed down?"

I MARRIED A TRUTH-TELLER.

Of course, I hadn't asked for her help and wasn't even open to her concern. But the question had an effect on me. I've thought about it, and she's right. I *would* feel better if I slowed down. And, although she didn't say it, I suspect I'd be a lot more fun to ride with!

Unexpected, unwanted questions open doors, don't they? When we are seeking to raise up leaders around us, we will need to welcome their questions—especially the ones we don't anticipate and don't particularly like.

Philip had the ability to identify and raise up leaders. We learn this especially when he heeded the voice of the Spirit and spoke to the Ethiopian eunuch in Acts 8:26-40. And we catch a glimpse of this ability in John 1:43-51.

Philip was called by Jesus. Philip responded both by following the Savior and by inviting his friend Nathanael. "Philip found Nathanael and told him, 'We have found the one Moses wrote about in the Law, and about whom the prophets also wrote—Jesus of Nazareth, the son of Joseph.'

" 'Nazareth! Can anything good come from there?' Nathanael asked.

" 'Come and see,' said Philip" (John 1:45-46).

Amazing. Faced with a question that would put most of us off, Philip simply accepted it. This led Nathanael to seek out the Savior to see for himself. Philip's nondefensive response to Nathanael's question opened the door for Nathanael to meet the one for whom he had longed, the Messiah.

And Nathanael's questioning didn't end with Philip. When he met Jesus, the Lord spoke of him in language that was both insightful and complimentary. The astonished Nathanael asked Jesus, "How do you know me?" (John 1:48). And when Jesus responded in a way that told Nathanael that Jesus knew he had been seeking the truth of Scriptures for a long time (theological discussions were often held under a fig tree), Nathanael responded in faith: "Rabbi, you are the Son of God; you are the King of Israel" (John 1:49). Then Jesus took the conversation to an entirely new level.

UNEXPECTED, UNWANTED QUESTIONS OPEN DOORS.

The point is that our Lord accepted Nathanael's question and, in so doing, opened him to a deeper calling of faith.

Effective leaders are willing to accept questions. This text teaches us that our willingness to receive even seemingly dismissive questions can serve as a door through which faith may enter.

When I was in seminary, one of my professors invited his students to his home for conversations about Scripture and faith. Those were some of the most remarkable learning moments of my life. His method was simple. He asked questions. His questions invited our questions. No matter how simple or ill-informed our questions may have been, he accepted them and, by his acceptance, invited us to consider the deeper truths of the gospel.

What's at stake when we do not accept the questions of others? Perhaps the question is best answered by another question. What might have happened to Nathanael if Philip had rebuked him for such a foolish question or defended his conviction that this Jesus of Nazareth was the Lord? Would Nathanael have had that remarkable encounter and conversation with the Savior that led to his faith? Probably not.

Christian leaders accept questions because we know that what is really at stake is whether the questioners feel acceptable. Philip understood that accepting the questions of Nathanael and the Ethiopian eunuch was the first way to show them that they were acceptable, not only to him but also to God.

Questions open doorways. They open doorways to personal growth, and, when understood and accepted by Christian leaders, they open doorways to God.

So I am not only going to practice patience when I drive, I am also going to start accepting the questions of others, no matter how silly they seem. Would you be willing to join me? I think such acceptance will open important doorways. And

I can't help but wonder what we might learn along the way and whom we might be surprised to find as companions in leadership. After all, Philip tolerated Nathanael's skeptical question, and look where it led.

LEADERSHIP PRAYER

Forgive me, O Lord, when my patience runs out and I can't tolerate another question. Remind me of Philip. Remind me of your own willingness to accept Nathanael's question. Then touch me with a small dose of your heavenly perspective so that I can see open doorways to you in questions I am likely to dismiss. Amen.

TEAM *Matters*

Objective: for leaders to understand that to raise up leaders means equipping them by answering *their* questions.

Items needed: a note card and a pencil for each participant.

CHALLENGE Give everyone a note card and a pencil, and invite participants to write down their questions about ministry, faith, or the Bible. Tell them they don't have to write their names on their cards. Give them plenty of time, and when they have finished, collect the cards and spend some time answering the questions. If there isn't enough time, commit to answering the remaining questions in writing and distributing the answers to the group at a future date.

READ Read John 1:43-51 aloud. In this passage, Jesus meets a skeptical man, Nathanael. Rather than trying to change his disposition, Jesus waits for Nathanael to open the door. Once he does, Jesus' answer profoundly affects him, and his viewpoint suddenly changes.

REFLECT Encourage participants to reflect upon this activity and the Scripture by considering the questions on page 107.

1. How did you respond to having your questions taken seriously?

- What happened when you heard the answers to your questions?
- Does having your questions answered help you become a more capable leader? Why or why not?
- How would you have responded if your questions had been deemed stupid or unimportant?
- How would you respond if your leader promised to answer your questions but never did?
- How does this activity translate into your position of leadership?
- How can you create an environment in which questions are acceptable?

Practice taking people's questions seriously this week. Note what happens when you do.

2. What's at stake when we don't accept others' questions?

- What's the price we pay for dismissing others' questions?
- Have you misjudged where your leaders are in their faith journey?
- How can questions serve as doors into people's faith life?
- Have you experienced such an opportunity? Describe it.
- When have you judged someone too quickly and been proven wrong later? What lesson did you learn from that experience?

Some people have leadership abilities but aren't using those gifts for God's work. In the upcoming weeks, look in all sorts of places for people with leadership abilities.

3. Think about how you currently equip your leaders.

- Are you the keeper of the information?
- Do you invite others to help in the equipping process?
- Do you make yourself accessible to your leadership?
- How does Jesus' equipping style as described in this story influence how you will equip in the future?

Commit to weaving some of these lessons into your next training opportunity.

21 TRUST THEM WITH THE MINISTRY

Mark 6:6b-13

"How many of you are non-staff members of churches?" I asked. I was addressing a group of nearly one thousand clergy and lay leaders of congregations in the metropolitan Chicago area. The majority of those present raised their hands.

"How many of you serve on committees or church councils?" I asked. Again, the majority raised their hands. "How many of you," I continued, "chose to get involved in your church to do the business of the church?" Almost every hand went down. "How many of you became active because you wanted to be a part of the ministry of your church and grow spiritually?" The hands flew up.

People no longer make a natural connection between the business of the ministry and the ministry itself. Many church members of previous generations assumed that the transactions of committees and boards were necessary for the ministry to grow. And for many years it worked. But more and more Christian leaders are experiencing what I experienced in Chicago that morning. Fewer people are willing to get involved in committees or even serve on church councils. Instead, they desire direct involvement in ministry.

CHRISTIAN LEADERS MUST STEP BACK AND TRUST THE LEADERS AROUND THEM WITH THE MINISTRY ITSELF.

There comes a point when Christian leaders must step back and trust the leaders around them with the ministry itself. Mark 6:6b-13 describes an instance in which Jesus did just this: "Calling the Twelve to him, he sent them out two by two and gave them authority over evil spirits" (verse 7).

The Twelve had been with Jesus for a period of training. They had seen him in action and listened to his teaching. They had also seen our Lord's ministry limited. The narrative in Mark that introduces this episode describes Christ's rejection by his hometown: "He could not do any miracles there, except lay his hands on a few sick people and heal them. And he was amazed at their lack of faith" (Mark 6:5-6a).

Interesting. The Twelve were sent out after they had seen the Savior's inability to do mighty wonders in Nazareth. Perhaps our Lord understood that their anxieties about their own abilities to succeed in the call would be lessened if they were sent out after they had seen him blocked by unbelief. The limitations of a leader can often be the doorway for other leaders to enter ministry—or, as in this case, to heed the call and engage in ministry.

This also would have established appropriate expectations for the work of the Twelve. Yes, they would experience miracles: "They drove out many demons and anointed many sick people with oil and healed them" (Mark 6:13). But they were also to anticipate the very rejection that Jesus had just experienced. When Jesus sent them out, he warned them to expect this and told them how to respond. "If any place will not welcome you or listen to you, shake the dust off your feet when you leave, as a testimony against them" (Mark 6:11). As they had seen their Lord rejected, they ought to anticipate their own rejection and not experience even the smallest sense of guilt or failure over it. The condemnation was not on them but on those who refused to hear.

Jesus also gave the Twelve specific instructions about provisions for their journey: "Take nothing for the journey except a staff—no bread, no bag, no money in your belts. Wear sandals but not an extra tunic" (Mark 6:8b-9). As the disciples had seen Jesus trust the Father for all he needed, so they were to trust in God's provision, not in their own abilities.

Sooner or later, Christian leaders must entrust those around them with the practice of ministry. This in itself is a fulfilling of our Lord's instructions to trust God. Only this time we are called to trust God to work in and through others. As God had, through Jesus, called the Twelve, so God would equip them. The equipping would be threefold. First, they were equipped by the gifts that God had already planted in them. Surely this is one aspect of our Lord's call to them in the first place. These were gifted persons who were called to follow the Savior. That led to the second manner of their equipping: They were given instructions. Finally, they demonstrated that the last way of equipping is by doing. We can learn to do many things in ministry only by actually doing them.

WE CAN LEARN TO DO MANY THINGS IN MINISTRY ONLY BY ACTUALLY DOING THEM.

I know that there are many reasons Christian leaders have a hard time handing off aspects of their ministries to those around them. One reason is that we often do the work ourselves more quickly and efficiently. Another reason is that we fear the consequences of failure. We worry about how failure will affect the one sent to provide the ministry as well as those being ministered to. But these fears have tragic consequences. By allowing our fears to limit our ministries, we not only stifle the gifts God has given other leaders, but we also shoulder the burden of ministry all alone.

Jesus sent the disciples out *two by two.* No one was to carry the burden of the gospel alone. I am struck by how rarely the New Testament records an instance in which a person is sent to minister alone. In the entire book of Acts, only Philip was sent out by himself to minister when he was led to the Ethiopian eunuch. Peter was always with others, as was Paul. God knows that we will learn more and be more effective as we share ministry with others. In order to do so, we must trust the God who goes with them and will lead them into the future into which they are called.

Jesus sent them out. He let them go and do it. When they returned, they could celebrate their obedience as well as their successes. I suspect there was a great deal of sharing and learning as the disciples debriefed with the Savior! So the role of Christian leaders is not only to call, teach, and send others into ministry; we must also help them learn from their experiences, just as Jesus did with the Twelve.

LEADERSHIP PRAYER

Lord Jesus, as you have entrusted the privilege of ministry to me, help me to equip and send others into the ministry as well. Forgive me when my own anxieties limit your raising up of new leaders for your church. Give me the insight to identify potential leaders, equip them as best I can, and then trust them and you to do what is good and healthful. Free your church from its fear of failure, and send us into the world you love. In your name, amen.

TEAM *Matters*

Objective: for participants to understand that, for leaders to succeed, they need authority as well as responsibility.

Items needed: newsprint, markers, Bibles, and a snack.

PREPARE & ASSIGN Before the meeting begins, have the ingredients of a snack, such as cookies and coffee, on site, but not assembled. Just as the meeting is about to begin, say that you must attend to another matter and will miss part of the meeting. Form three groups. Ask the first group to prepare the snack. Ask the second group to set up the supplies—newsprint, markers, and Bibles. Ask the third group to actually run the meeting.

DELEGATE Tell members of the third group that you anticipate being gone about thirty minutes and that in your absence they are to lead the larger group in answering two questions: (1) What is limiting our ministry? (2) How can we overcome those limitations? Ask them to record answers on the newsprint, and at the end of the discussion, read Mark 6:6b-13 aloud. Give the third group photocopies of the "Reflection Questions" on page 112, and ask them to lead the entire group through them.

EXPLAIN Return to the room as the group is wrapping up its discussion of the reflection questions. Explain that you were deliberately absent to illustrate that this story is about more than limitations; it's also about empowering leaders. Remind participants that Jesus did three important things in this story. First, he sent the disciples out in pairs; they did not go alone! Second, he gave them authority to do what he had done. And finally, Jesus gave them simple directions that may be summarized in two words: Trust God!

DISCUSS Ask everyone to find a partner and, in pairs, discuss the questions on page 113.

APPLY As the session ends, ask participants to consider their role as leaders. Will they accept the challenges facing their ministries? Can they move beyond the limitations they face and see a new future? Are they willing to step forward, in faith, ready to face rejection, powered simply by authority from God?

PRAY Finally, pray for the members of your team by laying hands on their shoulders and adapting the prayer on page 110. ■

REFLECTION *Questions*

Jesus sent out the Twelve on the heels of his rejection in his own hometown (Mark 6:5-6a).

- How might our limitations become launching moments for our ministry?

- What opportunity lies beyond these limitations?

- What is keeping you from reaching past those limits?

- Are you afraid of failure or rejection?

- Does it comfort you to know that Jesus experienced similar moments?

- How did Jesus react to this rejection?

- Did it stop him from pushing forward in his ministry?

- How does failure or fear affect our ministry?

- Reread Mark 6:11. What advice does Jesus give us when we face rejection?

How would you feel if you were one of the Twelve who were given authority and sent out to preach and heal?

- Would you be able to trust God enough to "take nothing for the journey except a staff [a walking stick]" (Mark 6:8b)?
- How can a person do ministry without any physical resources?
- What is Jesus suggesting with this command?
- Why is the fact that Jesus sent the disciples out in pairs important?
- Is this how you run your ministry?
- What resources do you rely on?
- What were the results of the disciples' work?
- What challenge does this present to you in your ministry?
- Will you give authority to your leaders?
- Will you send them into the heart of the mission to make a difference?

22 JESUS DIDN'T STAND ALONE

Luke 6:12-19

"Once you've worked in a team that really works, you'll not want to work alone again," she said. This teacher was telling me about moving into our school district from another state. In that state, she had worked in interdisciplinary teams. The teachers of language arts, social studies, and science all got together and planned lessons that connected with and built upon each other. The result was that they encouraged one another to better teaching and the students really learned. But such teams were not a part of the culture in our school district, and efforts to form teams were being met with mixed results. Her frustrations reached a boiling point when she invited another teacher to plan a unit with her so that their lessons would complement each other. The other teacher demurred, saying that it would take too much work and she would have to create a new set of lesson plans. "She just doesn't get it! Working together is so much more effective, and it's fun, too!"

Our faith in Jesus focuses quite rightly on the Savior. But we often miss the power of teams that Jesus demonstrated during his life on earth. There is a marvelous progression in Luke 6:12-19. First Jesus went up on a mountainside to pray. This solitary act connected the Savior to his heavenly Father. Then Jesus returned to those who were following him and selected the Twelve: "When morning came, he called his disciples to him and chose twelve of them, whom he also designated apostles" (Luke 6:13). After spending significant time in prayer, Jesus selected his team. These men would be closest to him, and he would send them out first to spread the gospel.

WE NOW LIVE IN AN ENVIRONMENT IN WHICH OUR FAITH CAN ACTUALLY ISOLATE US.

Next, Jesus "went down with them and stood on a level place" (Luke 6:17). Jesus stood on a level place. That may simply mean a level spot on the ground, or it might also be interpreted that the Lord now had a firm place to stand. He did not stand alone; he stood surrounded by his team. Surely this increased his confidence. His closest friends would support his teaching and healing.

Generations of American Christians assumed that our society was built upon and would reinforce the values of our faith. The Judeo-Christian ethic was firmly in place. The great stories of the Bible were considered truths that reinforced the ideals to which we ascribed. We now live in a different environment in which our faith can actually isolate us. One of the ramifications of this shift is that being a person of faith requires a sense of leadership. Christians who seek to live their faith will, sooner or later, be put into positions in which they will either lead from their convictions or give in to the pressure of cultural norms that no longer support their values.

OUR LORD DID NOT STAND ALONE—AND NEITHER SHOULD WE!

We need community. This remarkable episode in Luke's Gospel tells us that our Lord did not stand alone—and neither should we! We need each other. When we go through seasons of testing or doubt, we need to be reminded of the faithfulness of our God through the lives of other Christians. The Christian faith is not a private matter. It is profoundly personal, but it always calls us into community, into relationships that form faith-filled teams.

Not long ago, I went through a desert time in my prayer life. I was anxious about a number of concerns that had surfaced at church. Two important family issues also required my attention. (Why do these things always happen in bunches?) Consequently I was once again driven to my knees in prayer. But my prayers were met by silence. Nothing seemed to happen in response to my petitions. It seemed that a lot was going "up to God" but nothing was coming "down to me."

Then Marlene asked to meet me in my office. After the usual pleasantries, she said, "I don't know why, but I have been led to pray for you a lot lately. Is there anything going on that I could help you with?"

As a Christian leader, I tend to keep my personal problems and struggles to myself. But Marlene's question revealed that God had heard my prayers and wanted to remind me that I wasn't standing alone. God provided someone with whom I could share my struggles. The desert season of prayer was broken by the presence of another Christian. She became the presence of Christ for me, and when we prayed, she and I became the church together. I no longer felt as if I was climbing a mountain on my own. My feet had been planted on level ground. I had a place to stand that gave me confidence.

During his life on earth, surely our Lord needed the support of friends in whom he could confide. And, in so doing, he reminded us that we are social animals created by God to be in relationship with one another.

LEADERSHIP PRAYER

Dear Lord Jesus, you had to walk the final stretch of the road to the cross all by yourself. But I know that you had friends around you for much of your ministry. When I am going it alone, send me someone I can trust. Let me be open to your presence through the gift of another. If I can be such a gift to someone, give me the eyes to see the opportunity and the will to act on it. Thank you for all the ways you provide for me. Amen.

TEAM *Matters*

Objective: for participants to see that Jesus intended Christians to do ministry in teams and to understand how Jesus formed his team.

Items needed: a marble; a cup; one miscellaneous item per participant (for example, a ruler, some string, a book, tape, a block, a cup, a pen, a sheet of paper, a paper clip, a cardboard tube, a stapler); and a candy bar, a sheet of paper, and a pencil for each participant.

CHALLENGE Hand everyone one of the miscellaneous items you've gathered. Invite participants to work together to create a "machine" from these things. Show the group the cup and the marble. Explain that the goal is to design a machine that will enable the marble to travel from one end of the machine to the cup without falling off the machine. All of the items must be used in the machine. Tell participants that they'll have ten minutes to create the machine, and that if it is successful, everyone will get a prize.

REFLECT & DISCUSS Step back and see what happens. If the goal is achieved before ten minutes have elapsed, give everyone a candy bar. If not, call time. Then encourage participants to reflect on the activity by asking the following questions: "How did it go? What went really well? What didn't work at all? What was the hardest part? What was the easiest? How did you feel when it was finished? Did the time limit put stress on the process? Was the prize an incentive? How did these two things—the time limit and the prize—change your behavior? What leadership lessons did you learn from this activity?"

Distribute a sheet of paper and a pencil to everyone. Tell participants that you will read Luke 6:12-19 aloud and that you'd like them to jot down the verbs in the passage as you read it. Reread all the verbs aloud and ask participants what these words reveal about how Jesus chose his team.

Remind participants that Jesus spent the entire night praying before forming his team. Help the group see that if Jesus, the Son of God, needed a community to surround him in his work, it is likely that they do too. Encourage participants to reflect upon this Scripture and the activity by forming groups of two or three and discussing the questions on page 117.

If you didn't distribute candy bars earlier, do so now, even if the goal wasn't achieved in ten minutes.

Getting REAL

1. How do you choose your team members?

- Are you willing to recruit any warm body for your team?
- How often do you skip the prayer and discernment portion of Jesus' process?
- Do you lead your ministry from afar, or do you move among the people themselves?

Commit to using Jesus' process for choosing and working with a team. Choose one facet of the process, and focus on it during the coming weeks.

2. When have you needed a team?

- When has your team served as a community of support?
- Do you spend time in prayer with your team?
- Does your team stand together, united?
- How does your team handle conflict within the team?
- How does your team deal with criticism from others? In the face of such criticism, do its members still support one another?

With your team, create and commit to a covenant describing how the team will behave.

23 TEACH THEM WHAT REALLY MATTERS

Luke 12:13-21

I met George and Betty in Spokane, Washington. I was serving in my second congregation as an associate pastor. They had been faithful members of this congregation for over twenty years. Now Betty suffered from a debilitating bone disease. Her bones were literally crumbling within her body. She could no longer come to church, but George came every Sunday and, after worship, picked up a tape of the service to take home to her. One day he called and asked if one of the pastors could bring Communion to Betty. I had the time and made the visit.

As I entered their modest home, George spoke softly. "Betty is still sleeping. I'll wake her in a minute. Please come in; we've been expecting you, and I've got the coffee on." With that, I quietly sat on a chair opposite the sofa that had become Betty's daytime home. Soon George returned with two cups of coffee, which he put down on an end table near me. He turned to Betty and looked at her for a moment. I saw a look of love on his face that I have not forgotten. Then, more to himself than to me, he said, "Beautiful, isn't she?"

I looked at the small form on the sofa. This woman had shrunk five inches in height and was in her seventies. Then I looked at George again and understood. Love makes everything beautiful. I sat in awe at the presence of Christ, who had surely entered that living room unannounced.

Jesus taught his disciples what really matters. Luke 12:13-21 is a wonderful example of this truth. It begins with a plea for our Lord to arbitrate a disputed inheritance. "Someone in the crowd said to him, 'Teacher, tell my brother to divide the inheritance with me.'

JESUS TAUGHT HIS DISCIPLES WHAT REALLY MATTERS.

"Jesus replied, 'Man, who appointed me a judge or an arbiter between you?' " (Luke 12:13-14).

Why did Jesus refuse to get involved in this family dispute? It wasn't because justice wasn't at issue. Neither can we infer that the one requesting help was in the wrong. It was because Jesus wanted to direct attention away from material wealth to something much more important. He set before his listeners what really matters in classic rabbinical fashion by first stating the negative and then telling a parable that led to his positive point.

First he warned against the sin of greed: "Watch out! Be on your guard against all kinds of greed; a man's life does not consist in the abundance of his possessions" (Luke 12:15b). This was not a judgment on the case at hand; Jesus had already refused to get involved in it. Rather, Jesus warned his listeners not to get so caught up in a disputed inheritance that they were deceived into overlooking what truly matters. Then he told a parable to remind them that the things of this world will ultimately be taken from them. The final words of his parable direct our attention to God and the values by which God would have us live. Jesus said, "But God said to him, 'You fool! This very night your life will be demanded from you. Then who will get what you have prepared for yourself?' This is how it will be with anyone who stores up things for himself but is not rich toward God" (Luke 12:20-21).

What does this parable have to do with the original plea for arbitration between two brothers?

When my father and I went to my grandmother's funeral, I learned that he was the executor of the estate. My grandfather had died many years earlier, and the family farm had been sold. There were, however, a number of family heirlooms that my grandmother had kept. Some of these were of great financial value; others were of sentimental value. My father considered how to divide these things among his sisters and himself. He told me his solution: "The most important thing is that we remain a family. These things will come and go, but we will always be a family." So he wrote each item on a piece of paper and placed the papers in a box. Each person drew a slip of paper, and the item named on it became his or hers. If some chose to trade with others, that was fine. But my father was anxious that there be no quarreling over these things at the expense of the family members' love for one another. Everyone agreed, and the division of the inheritance went off without a hitch. The most important goal, the family members' love for one another, was honored and remained intact.

This is the leadership lesson I take from this text. The man who begged Jesus to arbitrate the dispute had put the inheritance above the love for his brother. He was in danger of committing the sin of greed, which always puts the things of this world above love.

GOD VALUES PEOPLE ABOVE THINGS—AND COMMANDS US TO DO LIKEWISE.

What really matters in the kingdom of God is love. God values people above things—and commands us to do likewise. Christian leaders who are committed to raising up other leaders for the ministry of the gospel need to continue to lift up the value system of heaven. Jesus took the very practical issue of an inheritance and elevated it. From the physical, our Lord spoke of the spiritual. From the temporal, the Savior drew attention to the eternal. The question we are left with is whether we will hold the things of this world in higher esteem than the eternal values of God.

The temporary gain of this or that ministry is of less importance than the presence of love. That's what I realized in the living room with George and Betty. Though sharing the Lord's Supper with them was important, it paled in comparison with the love manifested there. Even Holy Communion will one day give way to the nearness of the Savior in eternity. The activities and outcomes of our ministries will be held accountable to this much higher rule: the rule of love.

LEADERSHIP PRAYER

Lord Jesus, help me see your love in the things with which I fill my life. Help me see that what I do serves your love and that the activities of the church have value only as they extend your love into the real lives of others. And help me share this great truth with the leaders you've gifted me to raise up. Amen.

TEAM *Matters*

OBJECTIVE: to remind leaders of God's values and to help them discover their own core values.

ITEMS NEEDED: newsprint, markers, and—for each participant—a sheet of paper and a pencil.

CHALLENGE Give participants two or three minutes to find ten things in their purses, wallets, planners, and/or Bibles that represent what is important to them. Then ask everyone to find a partner with whom to discuss these ten items. What do they represent? Why are they important? What value do they represent?

READ & DISCOVER Invite participants to learn what God values by reading Luke 12:13-21 and to use the questions on page 121 to discover real wealth in their lives.

IDENTIFY Afterward, work as a group to create a list of values, writing them on a sheet of newsprint. Then ask participants each to write down *their* top five values and a sentence or two explaining their choices. Encourage participants to filter their decisions in the coming week through the values they've identified. ■

Enriching THE EXPERIENCE

This activity could also be used to create a list of core values for your ministry.

Getting REAL

1. Evaluate the ten items you chose.

- Do these items represent values of God or of the world?
- Can these things help you become "rich toward God"? How? If not, what would?

2. What are your sins of greed?

- How do these things take your attention away from God's values?
- Jesus said, "A man's life does not consist in the abundance of his possessions." How does that statement strike you?
- How would your life be different if you were not focused on possessions? What would be the most significant difference?

3. Reflect on Jesus' life. What were his core values?

- How did Jesus' values influence his decisions?
- Which of Jesus' values are core to you?
- How do those values help you in your everyday life?

24 SHOW THEN TELL
Matthew 9:35–10:1

My grandfather was a farmer. He lived through the deaths of two of his children and the loss of three family farms. He was starting to build a new life with my grandmother when my older brother and I first came to spend the summer on his Iowa farm. I would learn these things about him later in my life. What I learned about him very quickly was that he was a man of faith. He read the Bible every night, talked about God as if he really knew God, and was the first adult man other than a pastor whom I had ever heard pray out loud apart from mealtime prayers.

My grandfather talked about trusting God in all things. I believed him, but I didn't understand the depth of his trust in Jesus until one morning when he told me that the storm the night before had spawned a tornado and large hail. He was going out to see if the storm had damaged his field of soybeans. I asked if I could go along. When we got out of the car, we stood before a field of soybeans that the day before had been tall and green. Now their green leaves were pressed flat against the earth. It looked as if a herd of elephants had trampled those beans. The crop was a total loss.

I turned to my grandfather and asked, "Grandpa, what will you do now?"

Staring at the destroyed field, he replied, "Well, God will give us another year."

That was when I learned that his faith had to do with real life. In the face of devastation, he trusted God to provide.

THE BEST TEACHING SHOWS AND THEN TELLS THE LESSON.

Jesus knew that the best teaching shows and then tells the lesson. Matthew 9:35–10:1 describes our Lord's compassion for a bewildered people: "Jesus went through all the towns and villages, teaching in their synagogues, preaching the good news of the kingdom and healing every disease and sickness. When he saw the crowds, he had compassion on them, because they were harassed and helpless, like sheep without a shepherd. Then he said to his disciples, 'The harvest is plentiful but the workers are few' " (verses 35-37).

Jesus responded with compassion to the overwhelming needs of the people he encountered. He preached, taught, and healed. Then he turned to his disciples and told them that the need was great but the number of those who could help was few.

The disciples saw the desperation of the people. They saw Jesus' response. Surely they saw that the need seemed to grow rather than lessen. For everyone who was healed, three or four were brought to Jesus the following day. For every town or village that heard and received the good news of God's kingdom, three others remained without that knowledge. Jesus showed the disciples the greatness of the need, and then he showed them how to address that need.

After showing the disciples how to respond to the needs all around them, he told them to go and do it: "He called his twelve disciples to him and gave them authority to drive out evil spirits and to heal every disease and sickness" (Matthew 10:1). In other words, "As you have seen me do, now you go and do likewise." Having shown them how to do what they would be called to do, he now told them to go and gave them authority to do so.

TRUSTING GOD MEANS STANDING BEFORE A DEVASTATED PRESENT AND STILL ANTICIPATING A FUTURE WORTH LIVING.

I have never forgotten my grandfather's demonstration of faith that morning as he faced a wrecked field of soybeans. He showed me what he meant when he talked about trusting God. Trusting God means standing before a devastated present and still anticipating a future worth living.

The remarkable thing about ministry is that God provides models for most of us. In ministry, most of us realize that we have been open to the call because someone we knew or saw showed us how ministry could be effectively done. We have had the privilege of seeing ministry that mattered. The greatest sermons of all are the lives lived by God's saints in real time.

In the face of endless human need, the disciples must have realized that God wanted them to extend the work of the Savior for the sake of the people God loved. I can't help but believe that watching Jesus' ministry empowered them to say "yes" to meeting human need as well as "no" when it was time to step back from the brink of exhaustion. Jesus balanced love in action with love in contemplation and prayer. In this text, Matthew seems to be telling us that Jesus used the "show then tell" method of raising up leaders around him. No wonder they would eventually be willing to sacrifice their lives for him. He had given them his all. He didn't ask them to do anything they hadn't already seen him do. His teaching was always an extension of how he lived.

I have always wondered if I would be able to live out my faith before others as my grandfather did before me. I have prayed that God would give me opportunities to do so, especially with my children. As Christian leaders, we must seek to make our ministries an incarnation of our lives. The integrity of witness for which the world longs is found in the connection between who we are and what we do.

I hasten to add that this is not about perfection. Imperfect saints who live in forgiveness show others a tangible bridge between the gospel and real life. As we first claim and then extend God's forgiving love, we invite others to know the trustworthy

Savior on whom my grandfather leaned. And when all is said and done, that's what raising up leaders around us is all about.

THE INTEGRITY OF WITNESS FOR WHICH THE WORLD LONGS IS FOUND IN THE CONNECTION BETWEEN WHO WE ARE AND WHAT WE DO.

LEADERSHIP PRAYER

Heavenly Father, as the Savior first showed his disciples what to do and then told them to do it, may I show more of your love in my life. By the power of your Holy Spirit, let my words match my life and, when they don't, help me to claim your forgiving love. I ask that in my weakness and shortcomings your grace will be more clearly known. Let me show and then tell about this wonderful gift of grace you've given me. Amen.

TEAM *Matters*

Objective: for leaders to realize the importance of mentoring in equipping leaders.

Items needed: construction paper, pencils, scissors, tape, and markers.

Preparation: Cut out footprints from the construction paper, and write the names of great Christian leaders on them, one name per foot. Tape the footprints on the floor, creating a pathway from the doorway around the room.

CHALLENGE Ask participants each to think of a person who has influenced their leadership. Give each person a piece of construction paper, a pencil, and scissors. Have each participant trace one foot on the paper, cut out the footprint, and write the name of the person on it as well as one thing that person taught him or her. Place the footprints on the floor with the others.

SHARE Share a story that highlights a leadership lesson you learned from working alongside another leader. Note that most leadership is learned in the trenches through a lot of hard work and some trial and error. Demonstrate through your story that most great leaders don't aspire to greatness; rather, they see a need or opportunity, and they act.

READ & EXPLORE Read Matthew 9:35–10:1 aloud. This is a story of Jesus in the trenches. Point out how Jesus relied on his team to meet a need. Remind your leaders that as we raise up leaders, we need to remember that the main goal is to get them into the frontlines of ministry. Why? Because more than ever, "the harvest is plentiful but the workers are few." Use the questions on page 126 to help your leaders remember how they first started in leadership and to show them how they can engage others in leadership.

PRAY Have each participant cut out one more footprint and write his or her own name on it. Add these footprints to the path. Ask participants to take off their shoes and find a footprint to stand on. Close your time together by praying for the leaders who have influenced the members of your group, for the members themselves, and for those they will influence. Remind participants that this is holy ground and they are privileged to be a part of such a great group of leaders. Encourage them to believe that, together, they can make a dent in reaping the harvest!

1. Describe the first time you stepped into a leadership role.
- Did you feel prepared?
- Were you nervous?
- What happened? Did your first efforts go well, or did they flop?
- What about the second time? Was it different? better? worse?
- What did you do to get through those first times?
- How would you help someone experiencing ministry for the first time now?

2. Name several key characteristics you think are essential to be an effective leader in the church.
- Does your leadership reflect these characteristics?
- Share a leadership moment you will never forget. Why is that moment so important to you?
- What lesson did it teach you?

Ask three people you respect to share similar stories with you during the coming week.

3. Have you identified potential leaders with whom you should be spending time?
- What draws you to them?
- Have you told them about the leadership potential you see in them?
- How can they grow into their full potential?
- How might you assist them in reaching a new level of leadership?

Pray for God's guidance in contributing to these people's leadership development, then commit to contact these people in the upcoming week.

4. Are you in need of a mentor or coach?
- Who might serve in that role?
- If someone already serves as your mentor, how is it going?
- Is the relationship living up to its potential? If not, what's missing?
- Talk with the person about making some changes so that both of you might benefit.

Section Five
CONFLICT AND CHANGE

Two facts: (1) Leadership in any arena, including the Christian church, entails struggling with conflict and change. (2) Christian leaders cannot afford to be naive. Just as our Lord experienced these two realities, so will his followers. How can we face conflict and change with spiritual depth and confidence? How can we learn from them?

These devotions invite leaders to delve into the Bible to reflect on the unavoidable undercurrents of conflict and change. Sometimes the undercurrents flood into the open. Often they are silent sources of pain and challenge. But that we must deal with them is a certainty. I believe that we as disciples owe it to one another and our calling to speak of these things openly. Otherwise they can undo us, challenging our very calling as Christian leaders in the twenty-first century.

Conflict and change can actually enrich our spirits. Christian leaders will often learn the most valuable lessons of leadership as we struggle with conflicts we had hoped to avoid and change we may have either initiated or resisted. But if we choose to deny the existence of conflict and change, they can turn into demons with extraordinary power to defeat us and our ministries.

25 PRAISE, BLAME, AND THE LEADER'S INNER CONFIDENCE

John 12:1-8

I watched as she wheeled herself across the running track, past the weight machines and the well-proportioned people there. She passed the fitness desk and entered the next section of the fitness club. I couldn't tell if her malady was the result of a brain injury from an accident or an illness. In either case, this young woman had been robbed of a healthy, vibrant, normal body. Weaving through a room full of beautiful bodies, she sat as straight as her twisted body could in that motorized wheelchair. Her left foot was turned inward, her right hand bent at the wrist, and her smile slightly twisted. When her personal trainer greeted her, she lighted up.

"Can I help you out of your chair?" he asked kindly.

"No," she said with a slur. "I want to do it myself."

"Good for you."

Then I watched out of the corner of my eye as, for the next fifteen or twenty minutes, she fought a body that didn't want to perform. First one exercise and then another. First one stretch and then another. As her trainer talked to her, she responded in a voice that moved from determination to laughter.

Suddenly my exercise regimen was no longer daunting. The weights I was assigned to lift, not once but three times, were quite manageable. And I gloried in my aging but comparatively agile body. I marveled at this woman—her courage, determination, and spirit. With each exercise I prayed, "Lord, let this one be for her and others whose bodies can't do easily even what mine can."

Courage is the character trait I've come to admire most. While I admire the kind of courage that is demonstrated in war, the kind of courage that wins my heart is the grit to face one's limitations and refuse to give up. It was embodied in that young woman as she wheeled past all those fit bodies to begin a workout that pushed her to the max. I am awed by her strength.

Christian leaders also need strength, especially to face conflict. We may be praised for our ministry; we may be blamed. In the midst of such confusing and emotionally charged messages, how can we maintain our equilibrium? It must come from strength born of an inner confidence—courage.

In John 12 1-8, Jesus received in short succession a wonderful demonstration of love and honor and then harsh criticism: "Then Mary took about a pint of pure nard, an expensive perfume; she poured it on Jesus' feet and wiped his feet with her hair. And the house was filled with the fragrance of the perfume. But one of his disciples, Judas Iscariot, who was later to betray him, objected, 'Why wasn't this perfume sold and the money given to the poor? It was worth a year's wages' " (verses 3-5).

It would be easy to dismiss Judas' harsh criticism as a prelude to his betrayal. We might think that it simply shows how far from the heart of Jesus he had drifted. But I am struck by the language of this criticism. Isn't it true that those closest to us know how to hurt us the most? Judas knew Jesus' heart for the poor. He knew very well that Jesus valued people far beyond personal possessions. Judas' charge against Jesus must have stung, for it called into question the very integrity of the Savior's life and ministry.

THOSE CLOSEST TO US KNOW HOW TO HURT US THE MOST.

In sharp contrast, Mary's adulation must have felt wonderful to Jesus. Here was someone who understood his love and responded with an outpouring of her own love and regard. I believe this would have made Judas' criticism even more difficult to bear. Jesus, who so often set aside his own needs and desires for the sake of others, was charged with selfish indulgence by a member of his inner circle.

Jesus' response reveals an inner confidence that shows he put both the praise and the criticism in perspective: " 'Leave her alone,' Jesus replied. 'It was intended that she should save this perfume for the day of my burial. You will always have the poor among you, but you will not always have me' " (John 12:7-8). Jesus knew it wasn't really about him. It wasn't even about Mary. It was really about Judas, his greed and jealousy. But note how our Lord's confidence, even in the face of his certain death, led him through the praise, blame, and conflict.

Christian leaders learn early that criticism and praise come with the territory. And, disheartening though it is, the harshest criticism comes from those closest to us. They may call into question some of the very ideals we have sought to uphold and serve. If we trust God to be our final judge, if we are willing to learn from healthy and up-building criticism, then we will be able to respond to even the most painful criticism with a courage that comes from the Holy Spirit.

The young woman in the wheelchair got past people's stares because she knew what she was about. I thank God for her personal trainer. He encouraged her and treated her with respect. He was the "Mary" in that moment, and she the presence of Jesus. And I was a bystander who was profoundly blessed. When we as Christian leaders can pass by our critics with single-minded determination, as she did, we will end up blessing others. Some we will know; many will be strangers who have simply caught a glimpse of the Holy Spirit within us.

LEADERSHIP PRAYER

Lord Jesus, help me withstand the harsh criticism that is inevitable. And don't allow me to be seduced by the praise I receive. Grow within me your confident spirit. Amen.

TEAM *Matters*

Objective: for leaders to discover that their inner confidence is the anchor that helps them through good and bad times.

Items needed: a photocopy of the "Scenario" handout (p. 131) for each participant.

READ & DISCUSS Give each participant the "Scenario" handout, and read the scenerio as a group. Then, as a group, answer the reflection questions.

READ Read John 12:1-8 aloud. Draw participants' attention to the fact that this event occurred between the Pharisees' plotting to kill Jesus and his triumphant ride into Jerusalem on Palm Sunday—two contrasting and pivotal moments in Jesus' life.

EXPLORE With your group, unpack the context of this passage. Note the occasion. Jesus was with the family of Lazarus, whom he had raised from the dead. The family was hosting a dinner in Jesus' honor. Judas objected to the woman "wasting" expensive perfume on Jesus' feet. He didn't object to her interrupting the meal or her lavish response to Jesus. Judas viewed the situation strictly from a financial perspective. At this point Jesus made his point known. Ask participants to imagine the scene and Jesus saying, with an edge to his voice, "Hey, Judas, don't you get it? I've been teaching and preaching about unconditional love for months. I've called sinful and ordinary people like tax collectors and fishermen to be my disciples. We've walked through villages, healing the sick. I've raised people from the dead. And yet, as my days here are coming to an end, all you can think about is the price of this perfume." His real mission—to transform the human heart—had clearly been wasted on Judas.

Ask participants to examine Jesus' focus in this encounter. Here are some thoughts. Jesus' focus was on the Father. It is this focus that gave him the confidence to accept Mary's praise and to deal with Judas' criticism. Jesus was firmly grounded, anchored by his relationship with the Father.

REFLECT Conclude this session by asking individuals to consider what anchors their lives by reflecting on the questions on page 132 in pairs or small groups. ■

SCENARIO

Your church owns a plot of land adjacent to the property the church building occupies. A company that wishes to lease that land for the next ten years and construct a phone tower on it has approached your leadership. The price is good, but the contract is strict and demands high penalties for pulling out of it before it expires. Your ministry had planned to build a community youth center on that land in four or five years. Some people in your congregation have praised your leadership for its innovation in entertaining such a venture. Others have criticized your leadership for even thinking of partnering with a for-profit business. Your team is to bring a recommendation to the council at its next meeting.

Questions for Reflection

- What are the issues?
- How will you determine your focus in this decision?
- What process will you use to investigate the issues?
- What will give you confidence that you are making the right decision?

1. How do outward circumstances affect your life?

- Do you get caught up in the high and low points?
- Do they cause you to lose focus or direction?
- What gives you confidence during stressful times? Similarly, what helps you keep your equilibrium when things are going remarkably well?
- Are you building an outwardly focused life?
- Is time with Jesus a priority for you?

This week, be sure to spend time with Jesus each day.

2. Anchors, when in use, are invisible, yet they are lifesavers when storms come. Think about the storms you've encountered.

- What has served as your anchor during those times?
- How do you make sure that anchor is secure?
- What lessons can you learn from those times that can help you weather future storms?
- How does this anchor help you through tough times in your ministry?
- Can it help you maintain your equilibrium in times of praise as well?

Find something that symbolizes the anchor in your life. Carry it with you every day this week. Each time you are praised or criticized, let it remind you of the source of your security.

26 FROM THE MEAGER TO THE MIRACULOUS

John 2:1-11

I think I often suffer from bad theology. Oh, I've been to seminary and have benefited from some of the finest biblical and theological minds in this and other countries. It's not that I haven't paid attention. Nor is it that I've disregarded the teaching of these great women and men of faith. No, it's just that in the press of ministry, I slide into a theology of scarcity. When I weigh the options for ministry, I frequently become daunted by the costs. The costs may be measured in money, in demands on the time and energy of staff or other leaders, or in radically changing how these things are allocated. I begin to concentrate on all the reasons our meager resources can't possibly meet the challenges.

But the Bible consistently describes a God of abundance. Again and again in Jesus' ministry, the meager supplies of those around him were miraculously transformed into the abundance of God. The first miracle of Jesus described in John's Gospel is a case in point.

The story is well known. Jesus attended a wedding at Cana at which the host ran out of wine. This amounted to a social calamity! Jesus' mother asked for his help, and, though he initially demurred, he eventually responded with a miracle. He turned water into the finest wine.

Rather than simply creating wine out of thin air, the Savior transformed scarcity into abundance. He used a meager supply of water to demonstrate God's gracious abundance.

I have learned a great lesson, and this text confirms it: The only worthwhile vision for ministry is one that is so great that only God can do it.

THE ONLY WORTHWHILE VISION FOR MINISTRY IS ONE THAT IS SO GREAT THAT ONLY GOD CAN DO IT.

The world sees crises and all the reasons they can't be overcome. A theology of scarcity buys into this destructive perspective. As a consequence, we focus on the problem rather than the Problem Solver we worship. The practical ramifications of this faith dysfunction are many and all too obvious.

Many years ago, I had the privilege of leading a congregation in a building project. As the project progressed, we were faced with one financial crisis after another. We handled them all the same way: We scaled down the vision to match the scope of our own solutions. I can't recall once stopping in the midst of those considerations and praying that God would reveal the abundance of God's storehouse. We ended up with a blessing and an attractive addition, but we outgrew it almost immediately. Later I learned that this is a typical pattern in the church. We rarely build churches that are too large; we almost always under-build.

John records Jesus' miracle at the wedding to remind us that if Jesus can take common water from a village well and make of it fantastic wine, God can take the meager supplies of our lives and turn them into the abundance of heaven.

But we must be willing to act on faith. "Jesus said to the servants, 'Fill the jars with water'; so they filled them to the brim. Then he told them, 'Now draw some out and take it to the master of the banquet' " (John 2:7-8). The miracle depended upon the willingness of those servants to obey, at the risk of at least appearing foolish and perhaps embarrassing their host and enduring potentially disastrous personal results. But they did as they were instructed. They trusted this One who asked them to do what the world would have called foolish. They focused on the One who responded to their need. And their obedience resulted in a miracle.

WHAT IF CHRISTIAN LEADERS ACTED IN THE CONFIDENCE OF GOD'S ABUNDANCE?

What if Christian leaders—having tested their vision against the truth of God's Word and the best thinking of the discipleship community—acted in the confidence of God's abundance? Well, great cathedrals would be built in *our* time, in addition to the cathedrals that stand as relics of the patient faith of generations past. Justice would flow like water, not just reside as a memory of the risk-taking faith of the abolitionists of the eighteenth and nineteenth centuries or Martin Luther King, Jr. and Nelson Mandela of the twentieth century. And the hungry would be fed. I have heard it argued that the world cannot produce enough food to feed the world's hungry. But according to the November 22, 2002, Bread for the World homepage (www.bread.org), "Virtually every country in the world has the potential of growing sufficient food on a sustainable basis."

When I think of how those first Christians turned the world upside down, I can't help but believe it was because they trusted God's abundance to take their meager efforts and make of them the very kingdom of heaven. How can we dare less? Jesus calls us to see in the meager supplies and efforts that we present to him the very stuff of eternity. The miracle at Cana is an open invitation to see and trust the abundance of God in Jesus Christ.

LEADERSHIP PRAYER

O Lord of miracles, send your Holy Spirit so that I can trust in your abundance, not just in the afterlife but in the here and now. Forgive me when the world's perspective of scarcity blinds me to your abundant provision. Help me understand that your abundance will come in your time. God, grant me the confident patience to watch and wait for it…just as Mary did at Cana. Amen.

TEAM *Matters*

Objective: to remind leaders of God's miraculous provisions and encourage them to lead from a theology of abundance.

Items needed: a photocopy of the "Miracle, Coincidence, or Luck?" handout (pp. 136-137) for each participant.

CHALLENGE Give everyone a "Miracle, Coincidence, or Luck?" handout (pp. 136-137). Ask participants to evaluate each scenario and decide whether it's a miracle, coincidence, or luck. When participants have finished, ask them to compare their answers with another person's.

READ & REFLECT Remind participants that the Bible is full of descriptions of God's miracles, then read John 2:1-11 aloud. Encourage the group to reflect more deeply upon this Scripture and the issues raised on the handout by discussing the questions on page 138. ■

Miracle, COINCIDENCE, *or Luck?*

1. Your car breaks down on the highway, and you have forgotten your cell phone. Just as you are wondering whether you should walk to the nearest exit or flag down a car, a neighbor sees you on the side of the road and pulls over to help.

2. You haven't been feeling well for some time. Today the pain is too much, so you go to the emergency room. The doctors decide that you need surgery that afternoon, and your anxiety spikes. As you are being wheeled to the operating room, you meet the surgeon, who happens to go to your church. You tell her of your anxiety, and she offers to pray with you. Suddenly your perspective changes, and you are filled with peace.

3. Your daughter and her boyfriend spend the day motorcycling in the woods near your house. As they cross an old bridge, it begins to crumble beneath them. Caught in the middle of the bridge, they hear a voice say, "Hit the gas." They do and make it to the other side just before the bridge crashes into the river. They look around, but no one is there. Both say a prayer of thanksgiving and celebrate the gift of life.

4. In the final weeks of your maternity leave, you still are without child-care. You mention your concern to a co-worker who has stopped by for a visit. The co-worker's retired mother has been looking for work, and she mentions the need to her mother. The retired woman, wanting more details, calls you, and within two days you meet her and finalize plans for her to be your child's nanny.

5. Your family has had to move to another city in the middle of the school year, and you're worried about your children's school situation. On the day you buy your new house, you stop by the children's future school and run into a high school classmate you've not seen in years. You tell him your situation and discover he's a counselor at the school. He promises to help out in every way possible.

Miracle, COINCIDENCE, *or Luck?*

(continued)

6. The phone rings. Your spouse has been in an accident and is on the way to the hospital. You head to the hospital, where you discover that your spouse is unconscious and going into surgery. You call a friend and ask him to contact several friends and pray. Several hours later, the surgery is over, and the doctor reports that things are touch and go. The doctors have done everything they can; now all anyone can do is wait. You wait up all night but hear no news. In the morning, your spouse awakens, a bit groggy but basically all right.

7. Your office building is on fire, and you are trapped inside. The darkness surrounds you, and the smoke makes it difficult to breathe. As you are stumbling around, someone grabs your hand and leads you toward a door. Once outside, you turn and watch as the building collapses. Looking to your left, you realize the hand that guided you out of the building is that of a firefighter.

❖ ❖ ❖

8. Three weeks before the mission trip, two students are struggling to make their final payments. The father of one recently lost his job, and the other had to spend money on his car. Both have prayerfully considered their involvement in this trip and feel God has called them to participate, but they've exhausted their financial resources and are worried that they might not be able to go. You are just about to call them when a woman walks into your office and hands you a check for the exact amount the two owe. She explains that she prayed to find a recipient for this money and that she felt the mission trip seemed the right effort to support.

1. What's the "wine," or the problem you're facing, in your life?

- How might this be an opportunity for you to see God at work?
- How might your situation be an opportunity for others to see God's glory?

The result of miracles is that God's glory is revealed and the faith of others is increased. Who do you know who needs more faith? Write their names on a slip of paper, and attach it to your mirror. Pray for them every time you see their names.

2. Do you tend to focus on problems or solutions? Similarly, do you tend to focus on obstacles or on God?

- Define a theology of abundance.
- What changes do you need to make that will enable you to live with a theology of abundance?

Practice viewing life from this perspective. Obediently come to God with your needs, and see how God responds.

27 PRINCIPLES THAT WORK

1 Corinthians 8:1-4

"When people tell you that they don't like the direction of your ministry, it's usually not about the vision. It's almost always about tactics." Dr. Mark Zipper was addressing a group of leaders, and the question of managing conflict and change arose. "This is an important distinction. If the conflict is about tactics, this or that program, and the approach it is taking to a particular issue or need, then you can seek to redirect the individual to another aspect of the ministry that will serve the vision. If it really is about the vision and the changes necessary to implement it, then there are few options available. They will need to get on board or off the bus."

Conflicts about vision are among the few that cannot be resolved in ministry. That's because, like conflicts about values, we have to choose between them. Rarely can two opposing values be accommodated. And when it comes to vision, it's impossible to identify two different destinations and arrive at each simultaneously. But in either case, it is essential that Christian leaders understand the real issue.

In 1 Corinthians 8:1-4, Paul responds to a basic question by directing the reader to three great principles. Paul understood that if there was agreement on the three principles, then the issue itself could be dealt with graciously.

"Now about food sacrificed to idols...Knowledge puffs up, but love builds up" (1 Corinthians 8:1). The issue at hand—whether early Christians should eat food sacrificed to idols—is placed within the larger principle of love over knowledge. In Paul's time, almost all food was offered to a deity in symbolic gratitude. Then it was sold. Should the Christian, who believes there are no other gods, refrain from eating such food? Paul knew that there were those who claimed a special knowledge and on the basis of that knowledge set themselves up as authorities and demanded that Christians behave this or that way. Paul first levels the playing field: "We know that we all possess knowledge" (1 Corinthians 8:1b). Then, establishing that all Christians are on equal footing, he tells them that all are subject to the law of love, not specialized knowledge.

The first principle, then, is this: That which builds up an individual and Christ's church is the better good. All knowledge is subject to this great principle, just as all spiritual gifts (including knowledge) are given by God (1 Corinthians 12) and subject to love (1 Corinthians 13). This principle holds the particular, tactical issue accountable to the greater vision of God's love at work in and among God's people. Surely this is a principle that works in real life. I wonder how many conflicts within our ministries could be avoided or resolved if we held them up to the standard of Paul's principle of love.

KNOWLEDGE THAT IS FROM GOD IS IMBUED WITH THE WISDOM TO BUILD UP OTHERS.

The second principle is that knowledge is useful only when it serves to build up or unify the body of Christ. Unfortunately, knowledge often divides because it *puffs up.* Paul knew that possessing knowledge can lead people to assume authority where they really have none: "The man who thinks he knows something does not yet know as he ought to know" (1 Corinthians 8:2). In other words, knowledge that is from God is imbued with the wisdom to build up others.

Many years ago, the attendance at the church I was leading suddenly shot up. Six to ten families had come simultaneously from the same congregation across town. As I met with them and then with the pastor of that church, I realized that the primary cause of their leaving was the pastor's habit of talking about persons from the pulpit. Using his knowledge, he would expose the wrong in their opinions and actions. As I reflected on this, two things became clear. One was that if I had ever done that, I wanted to refrain from doing it again. The second lesson was that such behavior is unfair. Those about whom the pastor spoke had no recourse or ability to respond. When we have knowledge, it is tempting to use it to lift ourselves up at the expense of others, isn't it? That event in my early ministry was a strong reminder to hold myself accountable to two of the principles in this text: Act for love; hold knowledge accountable to the constructive ends that love promotes.

The third principle is the ultimate: "We know that an idol is nothing at all in the world and that there is no God but one" (1 Corinthians 8:4b). What a powerful statement! The conflict of loyalty between the Lord Jesus Christ and any pretender is false. There is simply no choice. We either believe in the God revealed in Jesus, or we believe in *nothing at all in the world.* The decision to eat the food or refrain from eating it is subject to the larger question: Will this action cause the faith in the one true God to grow? Because of this greatest principle, this tactical decision is a matter of individual discretion.

I was recently asked to preach a sermon on the devil. When I asked why, I was told, "Well, we don't hear enough about him in church. People need to know that the devil exists and is our enemy."

I thought about it and decided that, if a text suggested a conversation about the devil, then I would take the time to speak to the reality of this personification of evil. But I would never preach an entire sermon on the devil for two reasons. First, Paul's principle suggests that my sermons should be about the God who alone is

God. Second, I worry that some Christians are so frightened of the devil that they make of him another god. There is only one God. All the rest are lies or, as Jesus calls Satan, the father of lies. I am not sure that my tactical decision was the right one or the best of a number of right decisions. But it served the great principle that Paul articulates so clearly in this text.

Christian leaders can accomplish much by testing their decisions against principles that really work. The three that Paul mentions in this text are such principles. And we meet them again and again in his writings.

LEADERSHIP PRAYER

Almighty God, you who alone are God, bless me with a clear focus on the principle of love. I want my life and work to build up your people and your kingdom. Send your Holy Spirit to direct me toward that end in all I do. Amen.

TEAM *Matters*

Objective: to inform leaders of biblical principles for making decisions and give them practice in applying these principles to their decisions.

Items needed: a photocopy of the "Scenarios" handout (p. 142), scissors, and a hat or bowl.

Preparation: Cut the scenarios apart from one another, and place them in a hat or a bowl. (Make sure there are enough scenarios for each person to have one; more than one person may have the same scenario.)

CHALLENGE Have participants each randomly select a scenario and decide how they would respond to the scenarios they've chosen. Be sure to tell them there are no right answers! Then have everyone find a partner and explain how he or she arrived at that response.

READ & EXPLAIN Ask participants what criteria they use in making decisions. Point out that setting priorities for decision-making was a struggle for the early church, just as it is today. Read 1 Corinthians 8:1-4 aloud to discover the decision-making principles Paul suggests for our lives today. Highlight the three principles: (1) decisions should be based on love and building up individuals and the church, (2) knowledge is important only insofar as it is subservient to love, and (3) decisions must serve the one true God.

INTERACT In small groups, dig more deeply into these principles using the questions on page 143. ■

SCENARIOS

1 Two of your core values are family and faith, yet there are times schedules make it hard to honor these values. This week is no different. Sunday your family usually worships together, but your oldest son has a special hockey practice, and a close friend invites you to fill his final spot in a golf tournament. Your spouse wants the family to go to church, and you are concerned about what you are modeling for your children.

2 A member of your ministry team is spreading gossip. The first time you heard about it, you let it go. But now it has happened several times. You respect this person, but you see that the gossiping is taking a toll on your ministry. The group looks to you, the team leader, for advice.

3 You and your spouse have a once-a-month date night. Both of you cherish that time together. Tonight is your scheduled date night, but you have just received a call from a close friend whose child was just brought into the emergency room. She asks you to stay with her so her husband can remain at home with their other children. What will you tell her and your spouse?

4 Your leadership team is scheduled to cook dinner for new members this coming Saturday night. A friend at work just received basketball playoff tickets and invites you to go. You have known about the dinner for months and value the relationships with your team members, but you are also a big basketball fan.

5 Your daughter is in a school play and has invited you to come to her performance. You arrange to come, and she is very excited. The day before the play, your boss schedules an important meeting at the same time as the play. What will you say to your boss? What will you say to your daughter?

6 A friend from your couples' Bible study is having an affair. You and your spouse have a close relationship with this couple and are concerned. You are worried because the group meets at your house next week, and you wonder how you might make this into an opportunity to care for this couple.

7 You are a member of the youth ministry team, and a parent complains to you about the confirmation program. The parent complains that the church is asking too much of its students. (Students have been asked to participate in a service project and two retreats.) The parent feels these activities take too much time from an already busy schedule. A meeting has been called with the staff working with this ministry, you, and the parent. What will you say?

Getting REAL

1. "The man who loves God is known by God" (1 Corinthians 8:3). What do you think this means?

- What does this have to do with how we make decisions?
- How is accountability affected when we really know someone?
- Think of a close friend whom you cherish dearly. When you make decisions that affect that person, how are you accountable to him or her?
- When you love people, how does that influence your decisions about them?
- What are you willing to do to help those you love in their journeys?

Imagine you are as accountable to God as you are to the person you care most about. See how that perspective influences your decisions.

2. We are free to make our own choices, yet all choices have consequences. Some consequences affect us; others affect those around us. Some consequences are positive and build up the body of Christ; others are negative and tear down the body.

- How much energy do you expend weighing the consequences of your decisions?
- Do you focus on long-term or short-term consequences?
- How does this perspective enlighten your decisions? What happens when you've made poor decisions and hurt people you love?

This week, pay close attention to the consequences of your decisions.

3. Test some of your current decisions against Paul's three principles. How do your decisions stand up?

- Did you exercise love?
- Are you a support or a stumbling block to your brothers and sisters on their spiritual journeys?
- If you were graded on your decisions and your grade were based on these three principles, what grade would you receive?

Write these three principles down, and refer to them in the next few days as you make key decisions.

28 TIME TO MOVE ON
Mark 6:1-6

"I know that Schaller has said that a move can best be made when you come to the end of a chapter in your ministry," he said. "I have come to the conclusion that sometimes the question is whether you've bled enough for a ministry."

This pastor had led a conflicted congregation for some time. At least two previous pastors had crashed and burned in the same church. Two lay staff members had resigned midyear, and the congregation had begun to shrink. Now my friend was telling me that he was looking for a change. His wife was open to a move because she had seen the cost to her husband. For her, the decision was simple. "This ministry is not worth your life," she had told him.

Most Christian leaders will face the question of moving from one position to another. This is a difficult decision to make within the church. It may be just as difficult for Christian leaders outside of formal ministry, but rarely is it loaded with the spiritual implications that go with full-time ministry.

Jesus faced the same decision, and he decided to move on. Mark 6:1-6 describes Jesus' conflict in his home community of Nazareth that ended in Jesus' departure.

My friend moved as well. God blessed his decision with a congregation that welcomed and loved him and his family. But pastoral moves don't always end so well. Sometimes leaders move, not because they are clearly called, but because they seek to solve a personal problem on their own.

Jesus models for us the good reasons to move on. First, he taught those who gathered in the synagogue and made himself fully available to them. He spent time with the people. In the end, he knew enough about them to conclude that they would not accept his ministry because of their astonishing lack of faith.

When Christian leaders are confronted by rejection because of our message, it's probably time to move on. When we have spent time with those we have been called to serve and our work is greeted by a lack of faith, it is time to move on.

In Jesus' ministry, as well as in Paul's missionary journeys, I am struck by how often failure became the springboard to great achievement. When Jesus moved on to other villages, his ministry grew to the point that he sent out the Twelve because the need was so great and he wanted to extend his love beyond his physical limitations. When Paul was blocked by the Holy Spirit (Acts 16), he experienced the frustration of failure, which opened him to receive the dream and call to Macedonia. The Christians of that poor region were so transformed by the gospel that they became models of Christian generosity (2 Corinthians 8).

In circumstances like my friend's, failing to move would have made him unavailable for the harvest of the Spirit. His ministry had lost its passion. The lack of response had made a shambles of his staff. His health was at risk. And there was no real call of the Spirit to stay. By opening himself to the question of whether it was time to leave, he was asking two questions of God. The most obvious was "Should I go?" The less obvious was "Is there a reason, Lord, you want me to stay?" Whenever we are open to moving, we really are testing our call, our work, as well as the existence of other opportunities.

For our Lord, the door to Nazareth was closed. He moved on. This was his calling. We learn from him that there are times and reasons for leaving—without guilt—the ministries we are serving.

SOMETIMES LEADERS MOVE, NOT BECAUSE THEY ARE CLEARLY CALLED, BUT BECAUSE THEY SEEK TO SOLVE A PERSONAL PROBLEM ON THEIR OWN.

When I left a previous position, I experienced acute guilt. I was excited about the new opportunity to which the Lord called me, but there were moments when I felt so sad about the people I was leaving behind. Sometimes, when the excitement of the new ministry had waned, the lure of the old was enormous. I remembered faces, names, and situations that had mattered a great deal to me. In their place were the faces and names of strangers.

One evening I told my wife, Chris, about this. "Are you telling me that you aren't sure this is God's call?" she asked.

"No. I'm sure it is," I replied.

"Well, then, I'd say you are just grieving about leaving these people and this ministry. Isn't that the way it ought to be?" she asked.

Suddenly, I realized that I was actually feeling grief, not guilt. I know that grief is always a consequence of loss. Whatever the loss, we can always think of things we could have done differently. These feelings are important. They tell us that we have given ourselves to others and causes that mattered. But they shouldn't cause us undue stress or cause us to rethink our decision.

I don't know if the Savior experienced such grief or not. I haven't met a pastor or lay staff member who hasn't in similar situations. Yet God takes this grief and turns us outward, toward others in whom we can meet the Christ. And our ministries grow vibrant again.

LEADERSHIP PRAYER

O Holy Spirit, remind me to be open to your testing of my call. Help me not to run *from* anything but to run *toward* your call. Keep me connected to those I seek to serve so that, when I leave a ministry, it will be because there is more for me to do elsewhere. Amen.

TEAM *Matters*

Objective: for leaders to understand the importance of transitions and to help them determine what time it is in their ministries.

Items needed: a sheet of paper and a pencil for each participant.

CHALLENGE Give participants each a sheet of paper, and have them write "Table of Contents" at the top of the page. On the left side of the paper, tell them to list chapters (Chapter 1, Chapter 2, Chapter 3, and so on). Then ask them to think back on their ministries and divide them into chapters. For example, Chapter 1 might be titled "Wetting My Whistle: Folding Bulletins and Mowing the Lawn." Chapter 2 might be "Confirmation and Beyond: Making the Faith Mine." Chapter 3 might be "Testing the Waters: My First Paid Ministry Position," and so on.

When participants have finished, ask them to write down pivotal events and decisions in each chapter that moved them from that chapter to the next. (Perhaps the pivotal event was a move, a spiritual high, or the influence of a significant person, for example.) Ask them to note any themes that emerge.

READ & REFLECT Read Mark 6:1-6 aloud, then encourage participants to reflect on the factors that led Jesus to realize it was time to go. Note that teaching, preaching, and healing—the same three focuses of his ministry elsewhere—were not welcomed in Nazareth. His character was called into question, and the people were unable to put their faith in him and believe.

EXPLAIN Point out that ministry changes over time. Pastors change; people change; ministry contexts change. Change is not a bad thing, but ignoring it is! Tell participants that they can better deal with change if they pay attention to the transitions between changes. For example, when a student begins first grade, a parent should ask, "How is my child adjusting to being in school all day long and to the new demands being placed on her?" These are transition issues that come with change. Being alert to these issues increases our chances of adjusting to change.

EXPLORE Use the questions on page 147 to help participants determine if their calling is being fulfilled in their current ministry setting. ■

Getting REAL

1. Is God using you as an instrument in your current ministry?

- Are you opening yourself to God's call in your life?
- Revisit your call. How does it line up with your current situation?
- In your current setting, are doors opening or closing for your ministry?
- How would you answer the following two questions:
  - a. Should I go?
  - b. Is there a reason God wants me to stay?
- What impact would staying have on your spiritual life?
- Are you seeing fruits from your labor?
- If not, when was the last time you saw such fruits? What does this tell you?

Spend some time in prayer, confirming your current call or being open to accepting a new call.

2. Sometimes endings come without new beginnings. Have you ever experienced such a time?

- Did you walk away from one situation without another one in sight?
- Why might God have set this transition time aside for you?
- Our society does not always recognize our need for times of transition. What transitions are you experiencing?
- What do you need from this transition time?

Living in the unknown can be hard. If you are at this stage of your ministry, find someone you trust with whom you can share your experience.

3. How do you separate the grief that comes from leaving a ministry from the knowledge that you've been called to move on?

- What are some constructive ways you can deal with this grief?
- What will it take for you to enter into your new call emotionally healthy?

If you are experiencing grief, read about the stages of grief. Note where you are in the process, and get outside help if you need it.

29 RIGHTEOUS ANGER, COMPASSIONATE RESPONSE

Mark 3:1-6

When the Berlin Wall collapsed, the world was left reeling. No one had seriously thought that it would happen when it did, that its collapse would be so total, or that it would lead to the fall of the Soviet empire. The map of the world was redrawn in a matter of weeks. The geopolitical balance was shaken up. One superpower was toppled; another, whose confidence had grown over the years, was suddenly thrust into an entirely new role.

How did this happen? This is what I believe. I believe the causes are even more astonishing than the results. I believe the Christian presence in Eastern Europe contributed mightily to these events. The German Lutheran church in East Germany was substantially responsible for the collapse of that wall. In Poland, the Catholic church was largely responsible for the emergence of a new democracy. Prayer vigils brought the repressive governments of the East to their knees. Faith gave hope and power to the hopeless and powerless across that part of the European continent. God's patience seemed to have worn thin. God's will, which grinds slowly but exceedingly fine, worked in dramatic fashion—and the world changed.

JESUS WAS ASKING THEM WHAT KIND OF GOD THEY BELIEVED IN.

The Christian church has not always been at the forefront of social or political change for justice's sake. But there have been wondrous moments, including the civil rights movement of the 1960s and the shattering of apartheid in South Africa, when it has.

In Mark 3:1-6, we read of another instance in which God's righteous anger spilled out into the world. Jesus seemed to be quite aware of the attempts by the religious and political power brokers to trap him. Facing them head on, he raised the question of compassion and God's justice. "Jesus said to the man with the shriveled hand, 'Stand up in front of everyone.' Then Jesus asked them, 'Which is lawful on the Sabbath: to do good or to do evil, to save life or to kill?' But they were silent" (Mark 3:3-4).

Jesus was asking them what kind of God they believed in. Did they believe in a God who is more interested in rules or in life, in healing or in maintaining religious systems? We can imagine the stunned silence that settled on that synagogue. Any leader who has dared to ask antagonists the deeper question has known such a silence. These silences reveal the choice of belligerence over reconciliation.

That is when the Lord became angry. "He looked around at them in anger...*deeply distressed at their stubborn hearts*" (Mark 3:5a). His anger was a secondary emotion. His primary feeling was hurt; he was distressed by their lack of compassion and simple kindness for this man whose hand had withered. The opportunity to heal was present. Why should this child of God, who had suffered so long, have to wait another twenty-four hours for healing? The religious leaders' insistence on keeping their rules and systems rigidly in place blinded them to the suffering of others.

The righteous anger of God is always in response to the hardness of heart that is at the heart of injustice. But the judgment of God, as slow as it may seem at times, is as certain as the forgiveness that comes with repentance. When God's righteous anger erupts in judgment, compassion quickly follows. And that is exactly what happened in this passage from Mark: The man's hand was restored.

Many of us have been surprised when our compassionate acts or kind words were misunderstood. But in this text, Jesus' opponents used his compassionate response to justify their efforts to *kill* him. "Then the Pharisees went out and began to plot with the Herodians how they might kill Jesus" (Mark 3:6). We should not feel guilty or assume we've done something wrong when our actions of kindness are used against us.

Christian leaders know that God seeks healing and restoration. He does not intend the church to be used as a club that denies entrance to those who are judged ineligible for membership. That is what Jesus overturned in the synagogue that Sabbath. That is what God overturned when the Berlin Wall collapsed. God's righteous anger is surely that anger to which Christian leaders should aspire. At its heart, it is always about inclusion, healing, and love.

GOD DOES NOT INTEND THE CHURCH TO BE USED AS A CLUB THAT DENIES ENTRANCE TO THOSE WHO ARE JUDGED INELIGIBLE FOR MEMBERSHIP.

LEADERSHIP PRAYER

Lord Jesus, as you were angry with the hardhearted religious leaders in the synagogue on that Sabbath, give me the same kind of anger toward those who want to limit your compassion. Send your Holy Spirit to enable your church to work in your world for justice and mercy. And help me to be a part of that great work. Amen.

TEAM *Matters*

Objective: for leaders to learn about Jesus' appropriate anger and how to deal with this kind of anger in ministry.

Items needed: a photocopy of the "Christian Issues" handout (p. 151) for each participant.

CHALLENGE Give everyone a "Christian Issues" handout (p. 151). Form three groups, and assign one issue to each group. Have each group create a Christian response to the issue assigned to it.

SHARE After everyone has finished, ask each group to share its members' responses with the larger group.

Ask participants to talk about the things of this world that make them angry. Remind them that injustice exists everywhere, not just in Third World countries. Discuss some of those injustices.

READ & EXPLAIN Read Mark 3:1-6 aloud. Tell participants that this text is a reminder that our faith should affect our sight and that we may see injustices in our world that others do not see. Seeing these injustices may cause us to become angry. How can Christian leaders channel that anger so that it fuels a life of discipleship? Remind participants that Jesus always responded compassionately to victims of injustice.

REFLECT Invite participants to learn to channel their anger as Jesus did by reflecting on the questions on page 152. ■

Christian ISSUES

1

Affordable housing is an issue in your community. The problem is intensifying as more people struggle to find adequate housing. Several people within your congregation have organized in an attempt to improve the situation. This group asks you how the church will be involved. Your church currently provides emergency assistance and assists with local Habitat for Humanity projects.

2

An ex-convict has begun to attend your church. He has lived in the area for many years but has not been active in any church. While in prison he gave his life to Jesus and is looking for a place to connect with other Christians and make a new start. Someone in the community referred him to your church. Several of the leaders in your church come to you for help in deciding how to deal with this situation.

3

Homelessness is a growing problem in your community. The population that's being affected most is unwed mothers and their small children. Several Christian organizations in the area are hosting a meeting to address this issue. You have been asked to share a response that best articulates the viewpoint of your ministry. Your organization has been involved in several community efforts to address homelessness in the past with varying success.

Getting REAL

1. What angers you?

- Is your anger a constructive influence on your ministry?
- What are "righteous" reasons to get angry in ministry?
- What are compassionate ways of responding?
- What's important to remember when you're angry?

Consider the causes of your anger. The next time you're angry, remember to respond with compassion.

2. Is your ministry actively engaged in justice issues?

- Do the leaders of your ministry have eyes to see the injustice in the world?
- Are you developing leaders with compassionate hearts?
- Many of these issues are so overwhelming that a single leader or ministry can't change much. Yet as our numbers grow, so does our impact. How might you join like forces together?
- How might you begin to gain some momentum in righting the wrongs in our world?

In the months ahead, look for opportunities to connect people and/or teams with others who have similar passions.

3. Righting wrongs can be messy business. What's happened when you've become involved in such an effort?

- How have others treated you when you've welcomed those whom our society tends to disregard?
- God calls us to love our neighbor as ourselves. When has this been hard for you?
- How did you deal with the situation?
- What did you learn from that experience?

In the weeks ahead, be willing to get your hands dirty. Find at least one opportunity to let your eyes of faith lead you to right a wrong!

30 FROM COST TO BLESSING

Luke 9:18-27

"Well, how did it go?" I asked. The presentation was the first I had made before a large, multiethnic group. As I'd scanned that marvelous group of Christians, it had seemed to me that this was indeed a picture of the universal church. If an ethnic group wasn't represented, I couldn't think of which one. I was naturally anxious about how my message had been received. So I asked my friend Terri how it had gone.

"It was great!" she replied. "People kept talking about it, and they filled my workshop. They all wanted to know how to implement your ideas."

Christian leaders' efforts are often public. It's only natural to ask others to give us honest feedback. I felt both relieved and excited as I heard Terri's response. She's a truth-teller, so I could trust what she said. I needed her feedback because, when we share from our hearts, we can't objectively evaluate how we've done. We need others to critique us. I've also received other, not so positive, critiques that have been even more helpful.

In Luke 9:18-27, Jesus models the courage to ask how others perceive us: "Once when Jesus was praying in private and his disciples were with him, he asked them, 'Who do the crowds say I am?' " (verse 18). I have often wondered about this question. I believe it was an honest question that our Lord then used to open the hearts and minds of the disciples. But I also have wondered if, at this stage in his ministry, he felt a bit out of touch. Of course, he would have seen the crowds' response to his teaching and healing. But how did the people interpret his words and actions? Were they beginning to put all his words and deeds within the context of the Messiah or not?

I also wonder if Jesus was looking for reassurance. In his humanity, I suspect that there were times he depended on his friends, as I depended on Terri that day, to tell him the truth about how others were receiving his ministry as well as what they were saying about who he might be.

JESUS MODELS THE COURAGE TO ASK HOW OTHERS PERCEIVE US.

Christian leaders often wonder how we are being received and perceived. The courage to ask those we trust is one way to either reassure us or help us adjust our message and means. If one price of Christian leadership is public exposure, it's natural to want to know if the price is worth it.

I believe that our Lord's question, with its subsequent teaching, came as he moved from the intimacy of prayer with the Father into the public world of his ministry. Perhaps it was only in communion with the Father that Jesus felt really free from public scrutiny. His question to his disciples can be understood as his way of determining if the cost of ministry was worth it. Were the crowds getting it? What about the disciples?

" 'But what about you?' he asked. 'Who do you say I am?'

"Peter answered, 'The Christ of God' " (Luke 9:20). At least Peter got it. And he seemed to be speaking for the other disciples as well. If they understood that much, then perhaps they could hear the rest. Warning them not to tell anyone else, Jesus said, "The Son of Man must suffer many things and be rejected by the elders, chief priests and teachers of the law, and he must be killed and on the third day be raised to life" (Luke 9:22). Sometimes I imagine these words rushing from his lips. What a relief it must have been to say them!

But he didn't stop there. Jesus wanted his followers to know that they would also experience the costs and blessings of ministry: "If anyone would come after me, he must deny himself and take up his cross daily and follow me...I tell you the truth, some who are standing here will not taste death before they see the kingdom of God" (Luke 9:23b, 27).

The cost is that we must take up the cross. At least in part, the public nature of our calling is an aspect of the cross. As the Savior took up his cross, so are we to voluntarily accept the costs of Christian leadership. This is our way of honoring Christ with our own service.

JUST AS JESUS PAID THE PRICE AND RECEIVED HIS REWARD, SO SHALL WE.

Just as Jesus paid the price and received his reward, so shall we. We shall see the kingdom of God. And we are blessed to catch glimpses of Jesus' reign in this life, too. When we see a child beaming with the felt love of Jesus, we have seen the kingdom. When a teen discovers how he or she is valued by God and dares to make a public stand for faith, we have caught a glimpse of the reign of God. Whenever we see a marriage that has withstood the tests of time and that man and woman renew their wedding vows, we have seen the kind of commitment that is a sign of the kingdom of God. We realize that heaven isn't so far away. And the price is worth it.

So we speak to one another as those who understand the costs and blessings of Christian leadership. And like the first-century apostles and disciples of Christ, we encourage one another. It *is* worth it. Someday we shall enter into the reign of Christ and hear him say those coveted words, "Well done, good and faithful servant." That promise makes it all worthwhile, doesn't it?

LEADERSHIP PRAYER

O Lord Jesus, I long for the day when I shall enter into your kingdom. When I get tired and feel that the price of discipleship is too great, remind me of this hope and the promise of your eternal affirmation. And help me encourage other Christian leaders as your Spirit encourages me. Help me to dare to ask others how I'm doing and being perceived so that I can better serve you and lead others to you. In your precious name I pray, amen.

TEAM *Matters*

Objective: for leaders to reflect on the benefits and costs of their public faith.

Items needed: scissors and photocopies of the fake money on page 157 and the cards on page 158.

Preparation: Before this session, make enough photocopies of the handouts to give each participant one car card, one time card, three prayer cards, and ten $1,000 bills. Also make enough photocopies of the fake money to give yourself fifty $1,000 bills.

CHALLENGE Give everyone a car card, a time card, three prayer cards, and $10,000 in fake $1,000 bills. Tell participants that this is their resource pool. The car and time cards represent a participant's willingness to use these resources to help another. These cards may be used only once. The money represents the current balance in the participant's savings account. As the leader, you have $50,000 in the church's bank account.

EXPLAIN Read the following scenarios, one by one. After each, ask participants to decide how they'd be willing to help: with money, with prayer support, and/or with the use of their cars or homes. (Some may choose to use more than one resource on one scenario.) Have participants hand over the amount and/or the resource after each scenario is read.

READ Here are the scenarios.

- A big storm has damaged the roof of our church. As a result, rain and wind have destroyed the sanctuary. Because the insurance policy's deductible is extremely high, the church is left with a bill of $100,000.
- Your child is very sick. The only treatment that doctors believe will work costs $1,000 a month and is not covered by your insurance.

TEAM *Matters*

(continued)

- Your son has invited a boy in the neighboring apartments to come to the children's programs at our church. He is eager to attend, but his family is not able to provide transportation for him or pay the registration fee.
- A college student is interested in mission work. He is raising $2,000 for his first year and needs a place to stay for his one-month training session, which will be held at a neighboring church.
- A new ministry is being launched at our church. This ministry asks people to donate used furniture, repairs it, and then gives it to people in need. The ministry needs people to help transport and repair the furniture and a large, warehouse-type space to store the furniture. Space is available locally, but its rent is $500 per month. This ministry will not start until a site is secured and a team is formed.
- A factory in our area recently laid off over a thousand workers, so many families are hurting. The local food bank is desperately in need of food and volunteers. The food bank currently averages $2,500 worth of food per month and one hundred hours of volunteer time, but it's not nearly enough.
- A woman in our congregation needs dialysis three times a week. She is no longer able to drive herself to treatment, and her husband works too far away to drive her every time. A transportation service is available, but it costs $300 a week, and the couple can't afford it.
- Your sister needs treatment for alcohol abuse. She is currently without a job, and her husband's insurance will cover a twelve-week outpatient treatment program, but she is not able to get there on her own. There is also an inpatient treatment program in the area, but it's not covered by insurance. The cost to transport her to outpatient treatment is $100 per week. The cost of the six-week inpatient program is $5,000.

SHARE After all the scenarios have been responded to, ask participants to describe the experience. How did it parallel real life? How did they reach their decisions? What does it mean to be a public Christian today?

READ Read Luke 9:18-27 aloud, and ask participants to consider the costs of publicly living their Christian beliefs. Share with the group your ideas about what it means to be a public Christian.

REFLECT Ask participants to carefully consider how they're living as public Christians as they answer the questions on page 159.

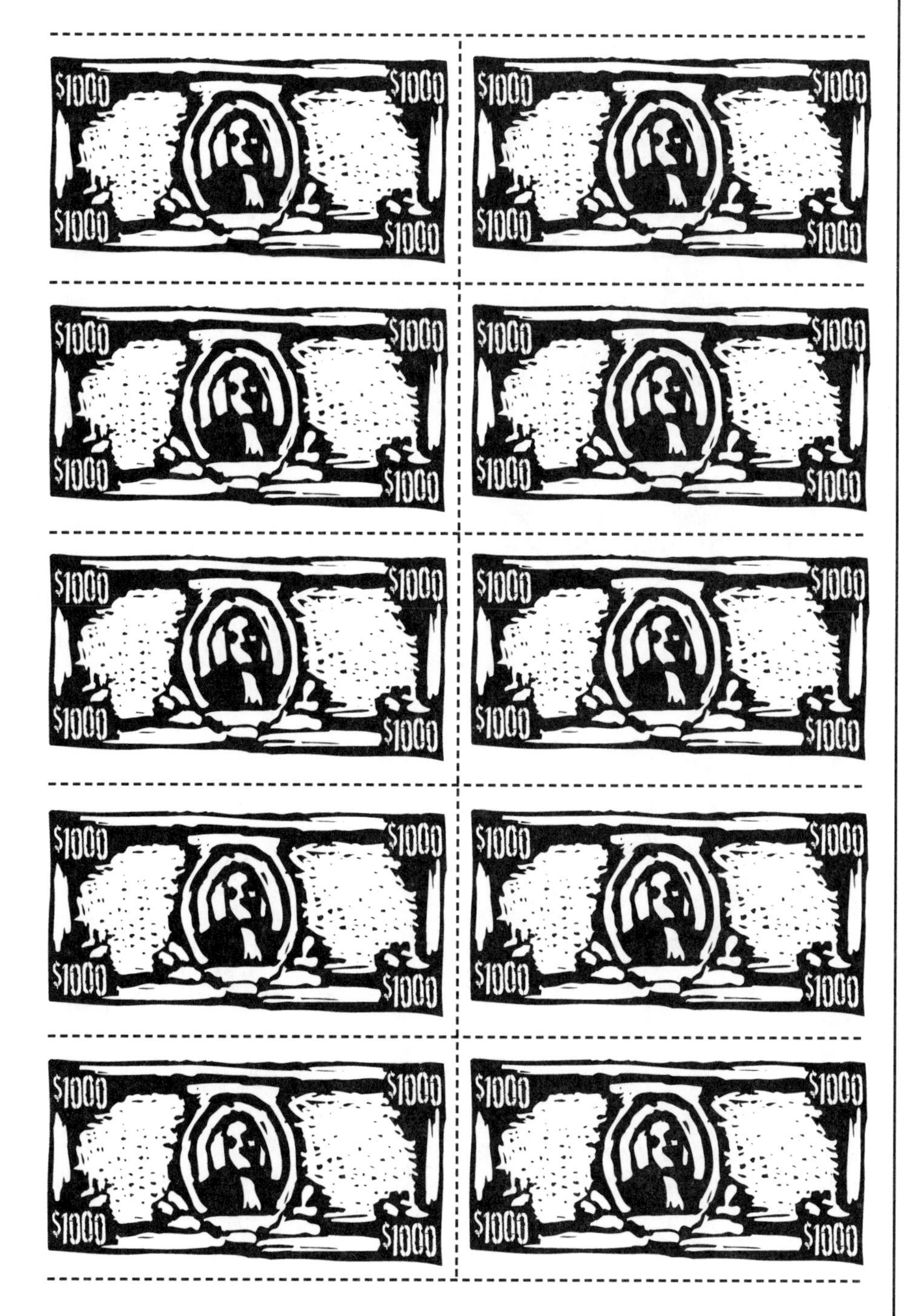
$1000

I will pray for you.

I will pray for you.

Good for two hours
of my time.

I will pray for you.

1. When has your public Christianity caused you pain?

- Have your sins ever been made public? Describe how you felt and responded.
- How were you treated by other Christians at this time?
- How were you treated by those not involved in a Christian community?
- What helped you through these times?
- How might you help others through such times?

Pray today for Christians around the world who are suffering because of their faith in Jesus Christ.

2. Each of us needs a thermometer for our ministry.

- Who can give you an honest reading of how people perceive your ministry?
- Have you ever sought the advice of others when the cost seemed too high?
- How did they help you discern God's plan for your life?

Write or call them to thank them for being present when you needed them.

3. Service is the currency of ministry. Are you operating from a conservative frame of mind or a generous one?

- What price are you currently paying?
- What benefits are you realizing?
- Which of your gifts is still untapped?
- How could you share your gifts?

Think about how you might invest your currency of service in ways that multiply your efforts.

4. When have you been privileged to see the blessings of heaven as a result of your work?

- How have you felt at those times?
- How was God revealed in those moments?
- What lesson have you learned from those experiences?

In the months ahead, make notes of those experiences in a journal. Refer to them when you need to be reminded of *why* you do what you do!

EVALUATION OF
What Really Matters

Please help Group Publishing, Inc., continue to provide innovative and useful resources for ministry. Please take a moment to fill out this evaluation and mail or fax it to us. Thanks!

1. As a whole, this book has been (circle one)

not very helpful *very helpful*

1 2 3 4 5 6 7 8 9 10

2. The best things about this book:

3. Ways this book could be improved:

4. Things I will change because of this book:

5. Other books I'd like to see Group publish in the future:

6. Would you be interested in field-testing future Group products and giving us your feedback? If so, please fill in the information below:

Name ______________________________

Church Name ______________________________

Denomination ____________________ Church Size ____________

Church Address ______________________________

City ____________________ State __________ ZIP __________

Church Phone ______________________________

E-mail ______________________________

Send to: Group Publishing, Inc. • Attention: Product Development • P.O. Box 481 • Loveland, CO 80539
or Fax: (970) 292-4370